The Cuban
Missile Crisis

Other books in the At Issue in History series:

The Cuban Missile Crisis

Loreta M. Medina, *Book Editor*

Daniel Leone, *President*
Bonnie Szumski, *Publisher*
Scott Barbour, *Managing Editor*
Stuart B. Miller, *Series Editor*

 **AT ISSUE IN HISTORY**

OPPOSING
VIEWPOINTS®
SERIES

GREENHAVEN PRESS
SAN DIEGO, CALIFORNIA

THOMSON
★
™
GALE

Detroit • New York • San Diego • San Francisco
Boston • New Haven, Conn. • Waterville, Maine
London • Munich

Library of Congress Cataloging-in-Publication Data

The Cuban Missile Crisis / Loreta M. Medina, book editor.
        p. cm. — (At issue in history)
     Includes bibliographical references and index.
     ISBN 0-7377-1121-3 (pbk. : alk. paper) —
  ISBN 0-7377-1122-1 (lib. : alk. paper)
     1. Cuban Missile Crisis, 1962—Sources. I. Medina,
Loreta M. II. Series.

E841 .C843 2002
973.922—dc21
                                                        2001051232

Cover photo: © Hulton Archive
Library of Congress, 56
National Archives, 23

Copyright © 2002 by Greenhaven Press,
an imprint of The Gale Group
10911 Technology Place, San Diego, CA 92127

Printed in the U.S.A.

Contents

Chapter 2: Exploring the Causes and Origins of the Crisis

describe their long struggle as a socialist state. Cuba was not a passive stage for the actions of the two superpowers: Cuban decisions affected how the crisis started, developed, and ended.

Chapter 3: Lessons and Revelations

president. To Sorensen, a leader's best tools in a tense confrontation with an adversary are his own judgment, knowledge, and willingness to negotiate with the other party.

Foreword

Historian Robert Weiss defines history simply as "a record and interpretation of past events." Both elements—record and interpretation—are necessary, Weiss argues.

> Names, dates, places, and events are the essence of history. But historical writing is not a compendium of facts. It consists of facts placed in a sequence to tell a connected story. A work of history is not merely a story, however. It also must analyze what happened and *why*—that is, it must interpret the past for the reader.

For example, the events of December 7, 1941, that led President Franklin D. Roosevelt to call it "a date which will live in infamy" are fairly well known and straightforward. A force of Japanese planes and submarines launched a torpedo and bombing attack on American military targets in Pearl Harbor, Hawaii. The surprise assault sank five battleships, disabled or sank fourteen additional ships, and left almost twenty-four hundred American soldiers and sailors dead. On the following day, the United States formally entered World War II when Congress declared war on Japan.

These facts and consequences were almost immediately communicated to the American people who heard reports about Pearl Harbor and President Roosevelt's response on the radio. All realized that this was an important and pivotal event in American and world history. Yet the news from Pearl Harbor raised many unanswered questions. Why did Japan decide to launch such an offensive? Why were the attackers so successful in catching America by surprise? What did the attack reveal about the two nations, their people, and their leadership? What were its causes, and what were its effects? Political leaders, academic historians, and students look to learn the basic facts of historical events and to read the intepretations of these events by many different sources, both primary and secondary, in order to develop a more complete picture of the event in a historical context.

In the case of Pearl Harbor, several important questions surrounding the event remain in dispute, most notably the role of President Roosevelt. Some historians have blamed his policies for deliberately provoking Japan to attack in order to propel America into World War II; a few have gone so far as to accuse him of knowing of the impending attack but not informing others. Other historians, examining the same event, have exonerated the president of such charges, arguing that the historical evidence does not support such a theory.

The Greenhaven At Issue in History series recognizes that many important historical events have been interpreted differently and in some cases remain shrouded in controversy. Each volume features a collection of articles that focus on a topic that has sparked controversy among eyewitnesses, contemporary observers, and historians. An introductory essay sets the stage for each topic by presenting background and context. Several chapters then examine different facets of the subject at hand with readings chosen for their diversity of opinion. Each selection is preceded by a summary of the author's main points and conclusions. A bibliography is included for those students interested in pursuing further research. An annotated table of contents and thorough index help readers to quickly locate material of interest. Taken together, the contents of each of the volumes in the Greenhaven At Issue in History series will help students become more discriminating and thoughtful readers of history.

Introduction

For thirteen days in October 1962 the world stood on the brink of a nuclear war. The Soviet Union had secretly deployed nuclear missiles in Cuba, ninety miles south of Florida. The missiles threatened not only major population centers in the southeast region of the United States but also the entire nation.

Outraged, the U.S. government immediately issued an ultimatum warning that if the Soviet Union did not remove the missiles, the United States would invade Cuba and destroy the missiles itself. U.S. president John F. Kennedy, in office just over a year, raised military readiness to the highest level throughout the nation and in its military installations abroad. Three hundred navy ships set sail near Cuba; three marine battalions were sent to the U.S. military base at Guantánamo on the southeastern coast of Cuba; missiles were set ready for launch; and twenty planes armed with nuclear bombs were ready to strike at targets in the USSR and in Cuba.

On the other side, the Soviets and the Cubans had at their disposal a sizable arsenal of nuclear weapons in Cuba. When the missiles were discovered, the Soviets had forty-two medium-range ballistic missiles that could strike at U.S. targets. Also ready for action were several jet bombers, jet fighters, air-to-air missiles, surface-to-air missiles, and missile patrol boats. In addition, the Cuban military—supported by 40,000 Soviet technicians and troops—had armed 270,000 people and had orders to fire on hostile aircraft in Cuban airspace.

Two superpowers confronting each other with nuclear weapons sent shivers across the globe. While President Kennedy and Soviet chairman Nikita Khrushchev negotiated, many people thought a nuclear conflagration was at hand. The situation was aptly described by Khrushchev himself when he said, "A smell of scorching hung in the air."[1]

Beginnings in the Cold War

In the United States, the crisis began on October 15, 1962, when the missiles were discovered by U.S. intelligence experts analyzing reconnaissance photographs. However, the origin of the crisis lay in the rivalry between the United States and the USSR, known as the Cold War.

Starting as an ideological struggle following World War II, the rivalry soon transformed into a race for military dominance. The quest for that dominance led to the development during the 1950s of nuclear missiles with ever-increasing range, speed, and accuracy. Statements by Soviet authorities gave Americans plenty of reason to worry. Soviet chairman Khrushchev announced, on various occasions, that the Soviets had the ability to "deliver a crushing blow against an aggressor,"[2] that "nuclear war . . . would result in certain victory for socialism."[3] In late 1961 Khrushchev publicly claimed Soviet military supremacy over the United States.

American Dominance

The reality was quite different. In October 1961 U.S. military intelligence discovered that the Soviet Union had exaggerated its estimates of nuclear strength. Authors Laurence Chang and Peter Kornbluh observe, for instance, that at the time of the crisis, the Soviets had only about forty intercontinental ballistic missiles (ICBMs), compared to over 170 U.S. long-range missiles, as well as 250 ready-to-fire nuclear warheads compared to 3,000 U.S. warheads.

The Kennedy administration exploited the new equation, declaring publicly that the United States had more nuclear weapons than the Soviet Union. In public speeches, U.S. officials made a point of underscoring America's military advantage. The revelation alarmed Soviet leaders. However, what incensed and tormented them was the encirclement of their territory by U.S. military installations in Britain, Italy, Turkey, and Greece. Equipped with nuclear weapons, these installations were all within striking distance of the Soviet Union.

Chairman Khrushchev would later cite the U.S. missiles in Europe as one of the reasons for his sending the missiles to Cuba. In May 1962, during a meeting with Soviet ambassador to Cuba Aleksander Alekseev, he argued, "Inasmuch as the Americans already have surrounded the Soviet

Union with a circle of their military bases and missile installations of various designations, we should repay them in kind, let them try their own medicine, so that they can feel what its [*sic*] like to live in the nuclear gun sites."[4]

In the end, U.S. warnings about the missile gap further fueled Soviet insecurity and inflamed the Cold War.

Cuba, an Active Participant

The Cold War, although dominated by the two superpowers, had another key participant in 1962—Cuba. Just four years earlier, Cuba had waged a revolution in which Fidel Castro had ousted the dictator Fulgencio Batista. Castro, who in the very beginning enjoyed support from the United States, slowly veered toward and eventually aligned himself with the Soviet Union. Cuba quickly became a pawn in the superpowers' rivalry. To the Soviet Union, Cuba was a model for socialism that should be saved from U.S. imperialism. To America, Cuba could open the way for Soviet expansion into South America.

At the time of the crisis, the Soviet Union and Cuba believed a U.S. attack was imminent. The 1961 Bay of Pigs invasion had floundered, but covert U.S. operations aimed at ousting Castro continued, causing Castro to believe a second attack was inevitable. Many years later former secretary of defense Robert McNamara acknowledged, "If I had been a Cuban leader at that time, I might well have concluded that there was a great risk of U.S. invasion. And I should say, as well, if I had been a Soviet leader at the time, I might have come to the same conclusion."[5]

Secrecy and Duplicity

To the United States, the missiles were unacceptable, but what had outraged American leaders was what they saw as Soviet duplicity. Before the discovery of the missiles, the Soviet Union had consistently denied it was installing offensive nuclear weapons in Cuba, asserting that Cuban stockpiles were defensive weapons only. A few days after the discovery of the missiles on October 15, Soviet foreign minister Andrei Gromyko—who, it has since been revealed, did not know about the missiles—assured President Kennedy that there were no offensive weapons in Cuba.

To respond to the crisis, Kennedy convened a group of his closest advisers, called the Executive Committee

(ExCom), which advised him of his options. Defense Secretary Robert McNamara outlined for Kennedy three courses of action: diplomatic engagement, naval blockade and air surveillance, and immediate air strikes to destroy the missile sites. Kennedy chose the naval blockade to stop the flow of more military supplies to Cuba. Soviet Ambassador Anatoly Dobrynin described the confrontation between U.S. and Soviet ships on October 24, when the blockade started, as the tensest moment of the crisis.

Secret Exchanges

During the first few days of the crisis, Kennedy and Khrushchev exchanged letters and conducted secret negotiations through their representatives. Finally, on October 26, Khrushchev wrote a letter to Kennedy offering to withdraw the missiles and military personnel if the United States publicly pledged not to invade Cuba. The United States was ready to accede to the proposal when it received a second letter from Khrushchev on October 27. The Soviet leader was now adding a second condition to the missile withdrawal. Not only did he want a guarantee that the United States would not invade Cuba, but he also wanted the U.S. Jupiter missiles in Turkey dismantled.

On October 28 tensions finally began to ease when Khrushchev announced that he would dismantle the nuclear installations and return the missiles to the Soviet Union, expressing his trust that the United States would not invade Cuba. Although tensions eased, the ordeal was not yet over:

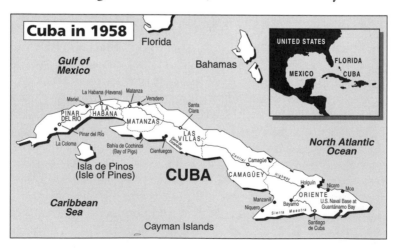

The two superpowers had yet to hammer out the details of the agreement and deal with Fidel Castro.

Factors That Helped Avert War

In their quest to prevent a catastrophe, several factors worked for both Kennedy and Khrushchev: their willingness to use diplomacy, to exercise restraint in the midst of pressure, and to give each other time to consider their options.

Although the two made it a point to talk and act tough in public, they secretly explored diplomatic channels to settle the stalemate. President Kennedy sent his brother and trusted adviser Attorney General Robert Kennedy to the Soviet embassy to discuss the issue privately with Ambassador Dobrynin. Again on October 27, after the United States received Khrushchev's appeal to end the crisis, the president sent the attorney general—without the knowledge of the rest of the advisers—to meet with the Soviet ambassador. It was at this meeting that Robert Kennedy offered to trade the missiles in Turkey for the missiles in Cuba.

It is to his credit that President Kennedy chose restraint. His was the voice of moderation among generals calling for quick and massive military attacks. Secret recordings, which the president himself activated during the Executive Committee meetings, show that he wanted to avert war. The same could be said of Khrushchev. In the aftermath of the crisis, he was ousted from office, but he earned the esteem of many world leaders for choosing to settle the crisis peacefully.

Robert Kennedy, writing in his memoir *Thirteen Days*, acknowledges the importance of time in the resolution of the standoff. The crisis played out over three weeks, and violence could have erupted at any moment. He notes that the Executive Committee met day and night to explore various options and debate the consequences. President Kennedy, who presided over most of the meetings, had the time to weigh the courses of action available to him. More importantly, Kennedy gave Khrushchev time to craft a response. For example, when he chose the naval blockade over quick air strikes, his limited action gave Khrushchev time to react.

Misperception and Miscommunication

Several factors encumbered the negotiations during the crisis and could have prevented a peaceful settlement. Among

these were the misconceptions and mistrust that compli-
cated the discussions of both sides. For example, at the
height of the crisis, when a spy plane was shot down in
Cuba, the Americans believed it was Khrushchev's move. To
them, it signaled a deliberate escalation of the situation. In
reality, however, the order had come from a Soviet commander, who might have been following orders from Castro, not Khrushchev. In fact, earlier Khrushchev had issued
strict orders to Soviet commanders not to take any action
that might provoke the United States.

Apart from mistaken assumptions, both parties had to
contend with the limitations of the slow-moving telegraph,
the fastest mode of transmission at the time. On October
23, after the first secret meeting between Robert Kennedy
and Ambassador Dobrynin, the latter had to send a message
to Khrushchev. He called a Western Union telegraph station, which sent a messenger on a bicycle to pick up his cable. Dobrynin urged the messenger to pedal back speedily
to the station. Again, on October 28, the letter from
Khrushchev—which offered to end the stalemate—had to
be broadcast simultaneously on Radio Moscow so that it
could reach the White House quickly. The Soviets feared
that at any moment the United States would launch an attack either in the Soviet Union or in Cuba. (Indeed, one
outgrowth of the crisis was the decision to install a direct
telephone link between Washington and Moscow.)

Mutual Responsibility

In the long run, in choosing to resolve the crisis peacefully,
Kennedy and Khrushchev realized that they had mutual responsibility for preventing a nuclear catastrophe, and that in
their hands lay not only the fate of their people, but that of
the rest of the world. The burden enabled the two leaders to
bring the most dangerous confrontation to a peaceful end.

Of this mutual responsibility, scholars James G. Blight
and David A. Welch observe,

> [Khrushchev] and Kennedy shared an awesome re-
> sponsibility in the Cuban missile crisis, a responsibil-
> ity no two men had ever had to share before. . . . Their
> joint responsibility for the survival of their nations
> and the peace of the world, and the powerful anxiety
> that accompanied it, overcame their ignorance, their

prejudice, their bluster, and their blindness, when it really mattered.[6]

Today, the Cuban missile crisis—claimed to be one of the most studied international confrontations of the twentieth century—offers an important lesson in global politics. Author Raymond L. Garthoff puts it succinctly, "What the Cuban missile crisis really demonstrated was that direct use of military force should not be resorted to when there are still diplomatic options for resolving a crisis satisfactorily."[7]

Notes

1. Quoted in Daniel Ellsberg, "The Day Castro Almost Started World War III," *New York Times*, October 31, 1987, p. 27.
2. Quoted in Laurence Chang and Peter Kornbluh, eds., *The Cuban Missile Crisis, 1962: A National Security Archive Documents Reader.* New York: New Press, 1998, p. 1.
3. Quoted in Richard Ned Lebow and Janice Gross Stein, *We All Lost the Cold War.* Princeton, NJ: Princeton University Press, 1994, p. 33.
4. Quoted in Lebow and Stein, *We All Lost the Cold War*, p. 48.
5. Quoted in Chang and Kornbluh, *The Cuban Missile Crisis, 1962: A National Security Archive Documents Reader.* New York: New Press, 1998, pp. 6–7.
6. James G. Blight and David A. Welch, *On the Brink: Americans and Soviets Reexamine the Cuban Missile Crisis.* New York: Random House, 1991, p. 312.
7. Raymond L. Garthoff, *Reflections on the Cuban Missile Crisis*, rev. ed. Washington, DC: Brookings Institution, 1989, p. 164.

Chapter 1

The Crisis Unfolds

1

The United States Discovers the Missiles and Warns the Soviet Union

John F. Kennedy

Six days after the discovery of the missiles in Cuba, President Kennedy tells the American people that he will not tolerate the deception by the Soviet Union and its deployment of the missiles. He informs them of the U.S. responses: a blockade, surveillance of the military buildup, retaliation in case of attack, and asking the United Nations to intervene. (Declassified documents would show later that while the president publicly chastised the Soviet Union, he privately explored diplomatic channels to resolve the crisis.) Kennedy was elected the thirty-fifth president of the United States in 1960. The youngest president in U.S. history, he was later assassinated in 1963.

(As Actually Delivered)

Good evening, my fellow citizens:

This government, as promised, has maintained the closest surveillance of the Soviet military build-up on the island of Cuba. Within the past week, unmistakable evidence has established the fact that a series of offensive missile sites is now in preparation on that imprisoned island. The purpose of these bases can be none other than to provide a nuclear strike capability against the Western Hemisphere.

Upon receiving the first preliminary hard information

Excerpted from John F. Kennedy's "Radio-TV Address of the President to the Nation," October 22, 1962.

of this nature last Tuesday morning at 9:00 a.m., I directed that our surveillance be stepped up. And having now confirmed and completed our evaluation of the evidence and our decision on a course of action, this government feels obliged to report this new crisis to you in fullest detail.

The characteristics of these new missile sites indicate two distinct types of installations. Several of them include medium range ballistic missiles, capable of carrying a nuclear warhead for a distance of more than 1000 nautical miles. Each of these missiles, in short, is capable of striking Washington, D.C., the Panama Canal, Cape Canaveral, Mexico City, or any other city in the Southeastern part of the United States, in Central America, or in the Caribbean area.

Nuclear weapons are so destructive . . . that any . . . sudden change in their deployment may well be regarded as a definite threat to peace.

Additional sites not yet completed appear to be designed for intermediate range ballistic missiles—capable of traveling more than twice as far—and thus capable of striking most of the major cities in the Western Hemisphere, ranging as far North as Hudson's Bay, Canada, and as far South as Lima, Peru. In addition, jet bombers, capable of carrying nuclear weapons, are now being uncrated and assembled in Cuba, while the necessary air bases are being prepared.

This urgent transformation of Cuba into an important strategic base—by the presence of these large, long-range, and clearly offensive weapons of sudden mass destruction—constitutes an explicit threat to the peace and security of all the Americas, in flagrant and deliberate defiance of the Rio Pact of 1947, the traditions of this Nation and Hemisphere, the Joint Resolution of the 87th Congress, the Charter of the United Nations, and my own public warnings to the Soviets on September 4 and 13. This action also contradicts the repeated assurances of Soviet spokesmen, both publicly and privately delivered, that the arms building in Cuba would retain its original defensive character, and that the Soviet Union had no need or desire to station strategic missiles on the territory of any other nation.

The size of this undertaking makes clear that it has been planned for some months. Yet only last month, after I had made clear the distinction between any introduction of ground-to-ground missiles and the existence of defensive anti-aircraft missiles, the Soviet Government publicly stated on September 11 that, and I quote, "The armaments and military equipment sent to Cuba are designed exclusively for defensive purposes," and, and I quote the Soviet Government, "There is no need for the Soviet Government to shift its weapons for a retaliatory blow to any other country, for instance Cuba," and that, and I quote the government, "The Soviet Union has so powerful rockets to carry these nuclear warheads that there is no need to search for sites for them beyond the boundaries of the Soviet Union." That statement was false.

Only last Thursday, as evidence of this rapid offensive build-up was already in my hand, Soviet Foreign Minister Gromyko told me in my office that he was instructed to make it clear once again, as he said his government had already done, that Soviet assistance to Cuba, and I quote, "pursued solely the purpose of contributing to the defense capabilities of Cuba," that and I quote him, "training by Soviet specialists of Cuban nationals in handling defensive armaments was by no means offensive," and that "if it were otherwise," Mr. Gromyko went on, "the Soviet Government would never become involved in rendering such assistance." That statement also was false.

Threat to World Peace

Neither the United States of America nor the world community of nations can tolerate deliberate deception and offensive threats on the part of any nation, large or small. We no longer live in a world where only the actual firing of weapons represents a sufficient challenge to a nation's security to constitute maximum peril. Nuclear weapons are so destructive and ballistic missiles are so swift, that any substantially increased possibility of their use or any sudden change in their deployment may well be regarded as a definite threat to peace.

For many years, both the Soviet Union and the United States, recognizing this fact, have deployed strategic nuclear weapons with great care, never upsetting the precarious status quo which insured that these weapons would not be used in the absence of some vital challenge. Our own strategic missiles have never been transferred to the territory of any other nation, under a cloak of secrecy and deception; and our history, unlike that of the Soviets since the end of World War II, demonstrates that we have no desire to dominate or conquer any other nation or impose our system upon its people. Nevertheless, American citizens have become adjusted to living daily on the bull's eye of Soviet missiles located inside the [Union of Soviet Socialist Republics] USSR or in submarines.

In that sense, missiles in Cuba add to an already clear and present danger—although it should be noted the nations of Latin America have never previously been subjected to a potential nuclear threat.

But this secret, swift and extraordinary build-up of Communist missiles—in an area well known to have a special and historical relationship to the United States and the nations of the Western Hemisphere, in violation of Soviet assurances, and in defiance of American and hemispheric policy—this sudden, clandestine decision to station strategic weapons for the first time outside of Soviet soil—is a deliberately provocative and unjustified change in the status quo which cannot be accepted by this country, if our courage and our commitments are ever to be trusted again by either friend or foe.

I call upon Chairman Khrushchev to halt and eliminate this clandestine, reckless and provocative threat to world peace and to stable relations between our two nations.

The 1930's taught us a clear lesson: aggressive conduct, if allowed to grow unchecked and unchallenged, ultimately leads to war. This nation is opposed to war. We are also true to our word. Our unswerving objective, therefore, must be to prevent the use of these missiles against this or any other country, and to secure their withdrawal or elimination from the Western Hemisphere.

Our policy has been one of patience and restraint, as befits a peaceful and powerful nation, which leads a worldwide alliance. We have been determined not to be diverted from our central concerns by mere irritants and fanatics. But now further action is required—and it is underway; and these actions may only be the beginning. We will not prematurely or unnecessarily risk the costs of worldwide nuclear war in which even the fruits of victory would be ashes in our mouth—but neither will we shrink from that risk at any time it must be faced.

Quarantine and Surveillance

Acting, therefore, in the defense of our own security and of the entire Western Hemisphere, and under the authority entrusted to me by the Constitution as endorsed by the Resolution of the Congress, I have directed that the following *initial* steps be taken immediately:

1) *First:* To halt this offensive build-up, a strict quarantine on all offensive military equipment under shipment to Cuba is being initiated. All ships of any kind bound for Cuba from whatever nation or port will, if found to contain cargoes of offensive weapons, be turned back. This quarantine will be extended, if needed, to other types of cargo and carriers. We are not at this time, however, denying the necessities of life as the Soviets attempted to do in their Berlin blockade of 1948.

President Kennedy informs the American people of U.S. responses to the discovery of missiles in Cuba.

2) *Second:* I have directed the continued and increased close surveillance of Cuba and its military build-up. The Foreign Ministers of the [Organization of American States] OAS, in their communiqué of October 6, rejected secrecy on such matters in this Hemisphere. Should these offensive military preparations continue, thus increasing the threat to the Hemisphere, further action will be justified. I have directed the Armed Forces to prepare for any eventualities; and I trust that in the interest of both the Cuban people and the Soviet technicians at the sites, the hazards to all concerned of continuing this threat will be recognized.

3) *Third:* It shall be the policy of this Nation to regard any nuclear missile launched from Cuba against any nation in the Western Hemisphere as an attack by the Soviet Union on the United States, requiring a full retaliatory response upon the Soviet Union.

4) *Fourth:* As a necessary military precaution, I have reinforced our base at Guantanamo, evacuated today the dependents of our personnel there, and ordered additional military units to be on a standby alert basis.

5) *Fifth:* We are calling tonight for an immediate meeting of the Organ of Consultation under the Organization of American States, to consider this threat to hemispheric security and to invoke Articles 6 and 8 of the Rio Treaty in support of all necessary action. The United Nations Charter allows for regional security arrangements—and the nations of this Hemisphere decided long ago against the military presence of outside powers. Our other allies around the world have also been alerted.

6) *Sixth:* Under the Charter of the United Nations, we are asking tonight that an emergency meeting of the Security Council be convoked without delay to take action against this latest Soviet threat to world peace. Our resolution will call for the prompt dismantling and withdrawal of all offensive weapons in Cuba, under the supervision of UN observers, before the quarantine can be lifted.

7) *Seventh and finally:* I call upon Chairman Khrushchev to halt and eliminate this clandestine, reckless and provocative threat to world peace and to stable relations between our two nations. I call upon him further to abandon this course of world domination, and to join in an historic effort to end the perilous arms race and transform the history of man. He has an opportunity now to move the world back

from the abyss of destruction—by returning to his government's own words that it had no need to station missiles outside its own territory, and withdrawing these weapons from Cuba—by refraining from any action which will widen or deepen the present crisis—and then by participating in a search for peaceful and permanent solutions.

Ready to Discuss

This Nation is prepared to present its case against the Soviet threat to peace, and our own proposals for a peaceful world, at any time and in any forum—in the OAS, in the United Nations, or in any other meeting that could be useful—without limiting our freedom of action. We have in the past made strenuous efforts to limit the spread of nuclear weapons. We have proposed the elimination of all arms and military bases in a fair and effective disarmament treaty. We are prepared to discuss new proposals for the removal of tensions on both sides—including the possibilities of a genuinely independent Cuba, free to determine its own destiny. We have no wish to war with the Soviet Union—for we are a peaceful people who desire to live in peace with all other peoples.

But it is difficult to settle or even discuss these problems in an atmosphere of intimidation. That is why this latest Soviet threat—or any other threat which is made either independently or in response to our actions this week—must and will be met with determination. Any hostile move anywhere in the world against the safety and freedom of peoples to whom we are committed—including in particular the brave people of West Berlin—will be met by whatever action is needed.

Finally, I want to say a few words to the captive people of Cuba, to whom this speech is being directly carried by special radio facilities. I speak to you as a friend, as one who knows of your deep attachment to your fatherland, as one who shares your aspirations for liberty and justice for all. And I have watched and the American people have watched with deep sorrow how your nationalist revolution was betrayed—and how your fatherland fell under foreign domination. Now your leaders are no longer Cuban leaders inspired by Cuban ideals. They are puppets and agents of an international conspiracy which has turned Cuba against your friends and neighbors in the Americas—and turned it into the first Latin American country to become a target for nuclear war—the first Latin

American country to have these weapons on its soil.

These new weapons are not in your interest. They contribute nothing to your peace and well being. They can only undermine it. But this country has no wish to cause you to suffer or to impose any system upon you. We know that your lives and land are being used as pawns by those who deny you freedom.

Many times in the past, the Cuban people have risen to throw out tyrants who destroyed their liberty. And I have no doubt that most Cubans today look forward to the time when they will be truly free—free from foreign domination, free to choose their own leaders, free to select their own system, free to own their own land, free to speak, and write, and worship without fear or degradation. And then shall Cuba be welcomed back to the society of free nations and to the associations of this Hemisphere.

My fellow citizens: Let no one doubt that this is a difficult and dangerous effort on which we have set out. No one can foresee precisely what course it will take or what costs or casualties will be incurred. Many months of sacrifice and self-discipline lie ahead—months in which both our patience and our will will be tested—months in which many threats and denunciations will keep us aware of our dangers. But the greatest danger of all would be to do nothing.

The path we have chosen for the present is full of hazards, as all paths are—but it is the one most consistent with our character and courage as a nation and our commitments around the world. The cost of freedom is always high—but Americans have always paid it. And one path we shall never choose, and that is the path of surrender or submission.

Our goal is not the victory of might, but the vindication of right—not peace at the expense of freedom, but both peace *and* freedom, here in this Hemisphere, and, we hope, around the world. God willing, that goal will be achieved.

Thank you and good night.

2

The President and Advisers Weigh the Options

Tim Weiner

For thirteen days and nights, President Kennedy listened to his closest advisers, sifting through layers of information, issues, convictions, and judgments in order to decide on a U.S. response to the crisis. While he listened to each and every one of the Executive Committee members, Kennedy secretly taped the discussions. The tapes, declassified and transcribed in the late 1990s, were subsequently released by the National Security Archive. Tim Weiner, writing for the *New York Times*, quotes from the 1997 book of Ernest R. May and Philip D. Zelikow, *The Kennedy Tapes: Inside the White House During the Cuban Missile Crisis*, which records the transcripts of the meetings of the Executive Committee while the Cuban missile crisis played out.

T his is how the world didn't end.
    On Sunday, Oct. 14, 1962, a U-2 spy plane discovered Soviet missiles secretly being installed in Cuba. Once armed with nuclear warheads, they could kill millions of Americans.

President John F. Kennedy had to decide whether to risk World War III over the crisis. He and his advisers met for 13 days and nights.

And he secretly taped most of the talks. The low-fidelity recordings, transcribed by Ernest R. May and Philip D. Zelikow, were published this month [in October 1997] as "The

Kennedy Tapes: Inside the White House During the Cuban Missile Crisis" (The Belknap Press of Harvard University Press). Ellipses in the excerpts below are from editing by *The New York Times* or denote unclear taped passages.

TIM WEINER

Tuesday morning, Oct. 16. Secretary of Defense Robert S. Mc-Namara has outlined three choices—negotiate, blockade or attack:

President Kennedy: There isn't any doubt that if we announced that there were [missile] sites going up . . . we would secure a good deal of political support. . . . This really would put the burden on the Soviets. On the other hand, the very fact of doing that makes the military . . . lose all the advantages [of a surprise attack].

McNamara: [MIG jets] could drop one or two or 10 high-explosive bombs someplace along the East Coast. And that's the minimum risk to this country we run as a result of advance warning.

Gen. Maxwell Taylor, Chairman, Joint Chiefs of Staff: I'd like to stress this last point, Mr. President. We are very vulnerable to conventional bombing attack, low-level bombing attacks, in the Florida area. . . .

Treasury Secretary C. Douglas Dillon: What if they carry a nuclear weapon?

The President: Well, if they carry a nuclear weapon. . . .

Secretary of State Dean Rusk: We could just be utterly wrong—but we've never really believed that [Nikita S.] Khrushchev [the Soviet leader] would take on a general nuclear war over Cuba.

The President: We certainly have been wrong about what he's trying to do in Cuba. . . .

McGeorge Bundy, Kennedy aide: What is the strategic impact [of the Cuban missiles]? How gravely does this change the strategic balance?

McNamara: Mac, I asked the Chiefs that . . . and they said, "Substantially." My own personal view is: not at all.

The President: What difference does it make? They've got enough to blow us up now anyway. . . . This is a political struggle as much as military.

The discussion turns to a "limited strike" to blow up the missile sites:

McNamara: You have to put in a blockade following any limited action.

Attorney General Robert F. Kennedy: Then we're gonna have to sink Russian ships. Then we're gonna have to sink Russian submarines. . . . [Think about] whether we should just get into it, and get it over with, and take our losses. . . .

Bundy: Our principal problem is to try and imaginatively to think what the world would be like if we do this, and what it will be like if we don't.

Thursday morning, Oct. 18. Should the United States warn Khrushchev before attacking the missile sites and killing Soviet soldiers?

Under Secretary of State George Ball: [If] we strike without warning, that's like Pearl Harbor. It's the kind of conduct that one might expect of the Soviet Union. . . . And I have a feeling that this 24 hours to Khrushchev is really indispensable.

This is a political struggle as much as military.

The President: And then if he says: "If you are going to do that, we're going to grab Berlin." . . . He'll grab Berlin, of course. Then either way it would be, we lost Berlin, because of these missiles. . . .

McNamara: Well, when we're talking about taking Berlin, what do we mean exactly? That they take it with Soviet troops?

The President: That's what I would think. . . .

Unidentified: Then what do we do?

Ball: Go to general war.

Bundy: Then it's general war.

The President: You mean a nuclear exchange?

Unidentified: Mmm-hmm.

Unidentified: That's right.

A little later, during discussion of an attack on Cuba, the President's brother speaks up:

Robert Kennedy: I think George Ball has a hell of a good point.

The President: What?

R. Kennedy: I think it's the whole question of, you know, assuming that you do survive all this, . . . what kind of a country we are.

Ball: This business of carrying the mark of Cain on your brow for the rest of your life. . . .

R. Kennedy: It's a hell of a burden to carry.

Friday morning, Oct. 19. The Joint Chiefs—especially Gen. Curtis LeMay of the Air Force, architect of nuclear strategy— want to attack:

General LeMay: If we don't do anything to Cuba, then they're going to push on Berlin, and push real hard because they've got us on the run. . . . This blockade and political action, I see leading into war. . . .This is almost as bad as the appeasement at Munich. . . . I just don't see any other solution except direct military action right now. . . . A blockade, and political talk, would be considered by a lot of our friends and neutrals as being a pretty weak response to this. And I'm sure a lot of our own citizens would feel that way, too. You're in a pretty bad fix, Mr. President.

The President: What did you say?

General LeMay: You're in a pretty bad fix.

The meeting ends. General LeMay and Gen. David Shoup of the Marines linger. General Shoup is impressed by the other's bluntness:

General Shoup: You pulled the rug right out from under him. Goddamn.

General LeMay: Jesus Christ. What the hell do you mean?

General Shoup: Somebody's got to keep them from doing the goddamn thing piecemeal. That's our problem. . . . Do the son of a bitch, and do it right. . . .

Monday morning, Oct. 22. President Kennedy asks Assistant Secretary of Defense Paul Nitze to make sure no American officer can fire nuclear weapons without the President's say-so:

The President: We may be attacking the Cubans, and a reprisal may come. I don't want these nuclear weapons firing without our knowing it. . . . Can we take care of that, Paul? We need a new instruction out.

Nitze: All right. I'll go back and tell them.

The President: They object to sending a new one out?

Nitze: They object to sending it out because it, to their view, compromises their standing instructions. . . . NATO strategic contact [jargon for a Soviet nuclear attack] requires the immediate execution of E.D.P. in such events.

The President: What's E.D.P.?

Nitze: The European defense plan, which is nuclear war. . . .

The President: No, that's why we ordered that. . . . And

what we've got to do is make sure these fellows do know, so that they don't fire them off and put the United States under attack. . . . I don't think we ought to accept the Chiefs' word on that one, Paul.

Monday, Oct. 22, 5 P.M. Before informing the American people of his plan for a blockade, the President briefs senior Congressmen. Senator Richard Russell of Georgia, the Armed Services Committee chairman, urges "stronger steps":

Senator Russell: The time is going to come, Mr. President, when we're going to have to take this step for Berlin and Korea and Washington, D.C., and Winder, Georgia, for the nuclear war. . . . We've got to take a chance somewhere, sometime, if we're going to retain our position as a great world power. . . .

The President: But it's a very difficult problem that we're faced with. . . .

Russell: Oh my God. I know that. A war, our destiny, will hinge on it. But it's coming someday, Mr. President. Will it ever be under more auspicious circumstances?

Saturday night, Oct. 27. A Soviet tanker keeps approaching the blockade. A U-2 is shot down over Cuba. The Joint Chiefs urge an all-out attack, which will start in 36 hours if the Soviets don't yield. The last recorded conversation that night:

McNamara: You got any doubts?

Robert Kennedy: Well, no. I think that we're doing the only thing we can do, and well, you know.

This is almost as bad as the appeasement at Munich. . . . I just don't see any other solution except direct military action right now.

McNamara: I think the one thing, Bobby, we ought to seriously do before we act is be damned sure they understand the consequences. In other words, we need to really show them where we are now, because we need to have two things ready: a government for Cuba, because we're going to need one. . . . and secondly, plans for how to respond to the Soviet Union in Europe, because sure as hell they're going to do something there. . . . I suggest it will be an eye for an eye.

Dillon: That's the mission.

Unidentified: I'd take Cuba back.

Unidentified: I'd take Cuba away from Castro.

Unidentified: Suppose we make Bobby mayor of Havana?

Monday, Oct. 29, 10:10 A.M. The crisis breaks. Khrushchev announces he will remove the missiles from Cuba. The President reflects:

The President: My guess is, well, everybody sort of figures that, in extremis, that everybody would use nuclear weapons. The decision to use any kind of a nuclear weapon, even the tactical ones, presents such a risk of it getting out of control so quickly, that there's—

Unidentified: But Cuba's so small compared to the world.

President Kennedy appears to agree.

3

Khrushchev Agrees to Remove the Missiles

Nikita Khrushchev

Soviet premier Nikita Khrushchev issues a communiqué to President Kennedy telling him that he has ordered the withdrawal of the missiles in Cuba, following the pledge of the United States not to invade Cuba. He brings to the attention of the American president the incursion of U.S. planes into the space of the Soviet Union and Cuba and asks the United States to stop these flights. He cautions Kennedy against starting a war and states his readiness to continue negotiations in the United Nations. Khrushchev rose to power in 1953, when he became the first secretary of the Communist Party, and ruled the Soviet Union until 1964 when opponents forced him to resign. He died in 1971.

(Premier Khrushchev's communiqué to President Kennedy, accepting an end to the missile crisis, October 28, 1962.)

Mr. President: I have received your message of October 27, 1962. I express my satisfaction and gratitude for the sense of proportion and understanding of the responsibility borne by you at present for the preservation of peace throughout the world which you have shown. I very well understand your anxiety and the anxiety of the United States' people in connection with the fact that the weapons which you describe as "offensive" are, in fact, grim weapons. Both you and I understand what kind of weapons they are.

In order to complete with greater speed the liquidation

From "Premier Khrushchev's Communiqué to President Kennedy, Accepting the End of the Missile Crisis," by Nikita Khrushchev, October 28, 1962.

of the conflict dangerous to the cause of peace, to give confidence to all people longing for peace, and to calm the American people, who, I am certain, want peace as much as the people of the Soviet Union, the Soviet government, in addition to previously issued instructions on the cessation of further work at building sites for the weapons, has issued a new order on the dismantling of the weapons which you describe as "offensive," and their crating and return to the Soviet Union.

Mr. President, I would like to repeat once more what I had already written to you in my preceding letters—that the Soviet government has placed at the disposal of the Cuban government economic aid, as well as arms, inasmuch as Cuba and the Cuban people have constantly been under the continuous danger of an invasion.

The shelling of Havana took place from a piratic ship. It is said that irresponsible Cuban emigres did the shooting. This is possibly the case. However, the question arises: From where did they fire? After all, they, these Cubans, have no territory, they have no private means, and they have no means to wage military action. Thus somebody put the arms needed to shell Havana and carry out their piratic actions in the Caribbean—in Cuban territorial waters—in their hands!

It is unthinkable in our time not to notice a pirate ship, particularly if one takes into account such a saturation of American ships in the Caribbean from which actually all this is watched and observed. In such circumstances, piratic ships are freely moving about Cuba, shelling Cuba, and carrying out piratic attacks upon peaceful transport vessels! It is, after all, known that they even shelled a British freighter!

In short, Cuba has been under the constant threat of aggressive forces which did not conceal their intentions to invade Cuban territory.

The Cuban people want to build their life in their own interest without interference from without. You are right in this, and one cannot blame them because they want to be masters of their own country and dispose of the fruits of their labor. The threat of Cuba's invasion and all the other ventures aimed at bringing about tension around Cuba are designed to engender uncertainty in the Cuban people, intimidate them, and hinder them in building their new life undisturbed.

Mr. President, I want to say clearly again that we could

not be indifferent to this. The Soviet government decided to help Cuba with means of defense against aggression—and only with means for purposes of defense.

We stationed defense means there which you call offensive. We stationed them there in order that no attack should be made against Cuba and that no rash action should be permitted to take place.

I regard with respect and trust your statement in your message of October 27, 1962 that no attack will be made on Cuba—that no invasion will take place—not only by the United States, but also by other countries of the Western Hemisphere, as your message pointed out. Then the motives which promoted us to give aid of this nature to Cuba cease. They are no longer applicable. Hence we have instructed our officers—and these means, as I have already stated, are in the hands of Soviet officers—to take necessary measures for stopping the building of the said projects and their dismantling and return to the Soviet Union. . . .

The Soviet government . . . has issued a new order on the dismantling of the weapons . . . and their crating and return to the Soviet Union.

I note with satisfaction that you have responded to my wish that the said dangerous situation should be liquidated and also that conditions should be created for a more thoughtful appraisal of the international situation which is fraught with great dangers in our age of thermonuclear weapons, rocket technology, spaceships, global rockets, and other lethal weapons. All people are interested in insuring peace. Therefore, we who are invested with trust and great responsibility must not permit an exacerbation of the situation and must liquidate the breeding grounds where a dangerous situation has been created fraught with serious consequences for the cause of peace. If we succeed along with you and with the aid of other people of good will in liquidating this tense situation, we must also concern ourselves to see that other dangerous conflicts do not arise which might lead to a world thermonuclear catastrophe.

In conclusion, I wish to speak of the regulation of relation between NATO and states of the Warsaw Treaty, which you mention. We have long ago spoken of this and are ready to continue an exchange of opinions with you on this question and find a reasonable solution. I also wish to continue an exchange of opinions on the prohibition of atomic and thermonuclear weapons, general disarmament, and other questions concerning the lessening of international tension.

Mr. President, I trust your statement. However, on the other hand, there are responsible people who would like to carry out an invasion of Cuba at this time, and in such a way to spark off a war. If we take practical steps and announce the dismantling and evacuation of the appropriate means from Cuba, then, doing that, we wish to establish at the same time the confidence of the Cuban people that we are with them and are not divesting ourselves of the responsibility of granting help to them.

We are convinced that the people of all countries, like yourself, Mr. President, will understand me correctly, we do not issue threats. We desire only peace. . . .

I should like, Mr. President, to remind you that military aircraft of a reconnaissance character have violated the frontier of the Soviet Union in connection with which we had conflicts with you. An exchange of notes took place.

In 1960, we shot down your U-2 aircraft, the reconnaissance flight of which over the USSR led to the wrecking of the meeting of the powers in Paris. You then took a correct position in condemning that criminal action by the former United States government. However, during the period of your tenure of office as president, a second instance of the violation of our frontier by an American U-2 aircraft took place in the Sakhalin area. We wrote you about this violation on August 30. You replied that this violation had taken place as the result of bad weather and gave an assurance that it would not be repeated. We gave credence to your assurance because there was indeed bad weather in that area at that time. However, if your aircraft did not have the task of flying near our territory, then even bad weather could not cause an American aircraft to enter our airspace.

The conclusion follows from this that it is done with the knowledge of the Pentagon, which tramples on international practices and violates the frontiers of other states.

An even more dangerous case occurred on October 23 when your reconnaissance aircraft intruded into the territory of the Soviet Union in the north, in the area of the Chukotka peninsula, and flew over our territory.

One asks, Mr. President, how should we regard this? What is it? A provocation? Your aircraft violates our frontier and at times as anxious as those which we are now experiencing when everything has been placed in a state of combat readiness, for an intruding American aircraft can easily be taken for a bomber with nuclear weapons, and this could push us toward a fatal step—all the more so because both the United States government and Pentagon have long been saying that bombers with atomic bombs are constantly on duty in your country. . . .

I would like to ask you to assess this correctly and take steps accordingly in order that it would not serve as a provocation for unleashing war.

I regard with respect and trust your statement
. . . of October 27, 1962 that no attack will be
made on Cuba—that no invasion will take place.

I would also like to express the following wish. Of course, it is a matter for the Cuban people. You do not at present maintain any diplomatic relations but through my officers on Cuba I have reports that flights of American aircraft over Cuba are being carried out. We are interested that there should not be any war at all in the world, and that the Cuban people should live quietly. However, Mr. President, it is no secret that we have our people on Cuba. According to the treaty with the Cuban government, we have officers and instructors there who are training the Cubans. They are mainly ordinary people—experts, agronomists, zootechnicians, irrigation and soil improvement experts, ordinary workers, tractor drivers, and others. We are concerned about them.

I would like to ask you, Mr. President, to bear in mind that a violation of Cuban airspace by American aircraft may also have dangerous consequences. If you do not want this, then no pretext should be given for the creation of a dangerous situation.

We must be now very cautious and not take such steps which will be of no use for the defense of the states involved in the conflict, but which are likely to arouse only irritation and even prove a provocation leading to the baneful step. We must, therefore, display a sobriety and wisdom and refrain from steps of this sort.

We value peace, perhaps even more than other people, because we experienced the terrible war against Hitler. However, our people will not flinch in the face of any ordeal. Our people trust their government, and we assure our people and the world public that the Soviet government will not allow itself to be provoked.

Should the provocateurs unleash a war, they would not escape the grave consequences of such a war. However, we are confident that reason will triumph. War will not be unleashed and the peace and security of people will be insured!

In connection with negotiations in progress between U.N. Acting Secretary General U Thant and representatives of the Soviet Union, the United States, and the Cuban Republic, the Soviet government has sent to New York USSR First Deputy Minister of Foreign Affairs Kuznetsov with a view to assisting U Thant in his noble efforts aimed at liquidation of the present dangerous situation.

With respect for you, Khrushchev. October 28, 1962.

Chapter 2

Exploring the Causes and Origins of the Crisis

1

Cold War Tensions Led to the Cuban Missile Crisis

Laurence Chang and Peter Kornbluh

The authors trace the origins of the Cuban missile crisis to the conflicted relationship between the two superpowers, as well as the United States' engagement in Cuba. For many years, the U.S. government maintained it never planned to invade Cuba in October 1962 before the missile crisis broke out. However, recently declassified information shows that as early as November 1961, the Kennedy administration had devised plans to intervene militarily in Cuba, assassinate Fidel Castro, and install a favorable government in Havana. According to the authors, this has validated Khrushchev's claim that the missiles were purely for Cuba's defense. At the time of writing, Laurence Chang was project director for the National Security Archive's declassified information on the Cuban missile crisis. He is the author and editor of several works on the missile crisis. Peter Kornbluh was director of the Cuba Documentation Project at the National Security Archive, while teaching at Columbia University's School of International and Public Affairs. He is coeditor of *The Politics of Illusion: The Bay of Pigs Reexamined* and *The Iran-Contra Scandal: The Declassified History*.

In April 1962, Soviet Premier Nikita Khrushchev first considered the idea of deploying nuclear missiles on the Caribbean island of Cuba. Over the next few weeks, Khrushchev would discuss this dangerous proposition with key advisers, and in May he dispatched the head of Soviet Strategic Rocket Forces, Marshall Sergei Biryuzov—traveling incognito as a member of an agricultural delegation—to confer with Cuban leader Fidel Castro and determine whether the missiles could be installed without detection by U.S. intelligence. When in early June Biryuzov reported back that Castro had responded positively to the Soviet proposal, and that clandestine installation was possible, Khrushchev ordered the project to proceed. By early September, shipments of equipment, materials, and weapon parts for deploying some forty-two SS-4 medium range ballistic missiles (MRBMs) and thirty-two SS-5 intermediate-range ballistic missiles (IRBMs) began arriving in Cuba.

What caused the Cuban missile crisis? Only a partial answer to this question can be found in the series of extraordinary decisions made by Soviet and Cuban leaders in the spring and summer of 1962; for Khrushchev's decision to deploy the missiles, and Castro's decision to accept them, did not take place in a vacuum. While their plan to secretly install nuclear missiles in Cuba was a bold and reckless *initiative*, it also represented a *response* to the underlying military and political tensions that characterized relations between Washington, Moscow, and Havana at the beginning of the 1960s. The origins of the missile crisis, therefore, can be found in the Cold War dynamic between the United States and the Soviet Union, and in the United States' hostile policy toward the Cuban revolution.

The United States and the Soviet Union

U.S.-Soviet relations in the period preceding the missile crisis were characterized by recurring conflict. Many issues, including the accelerating nuclear arms race, U.S. deployment of nuclear weapons along the Soviet periphery, Soviet support for revolution in the Third World, and most important, the unresolved status of Berlin, inflamed superpower tensions and sustained fears on both sides that the Cold War might escalate into some form of open military conflict.

Nuclear weapons rendered such conflict exceedingly dangerous. The Soviets had launched Sputnik in 1957 and Khrushchev began to rattle his atomic sabers, referring publicly to the Soviets' ability to "deliver a crushing blow" against an aggressor on any part of the globe, and raising concerns in Washington that the Soviet Union was developing a dangerous nuclear advantage. Perceptions of a "missile gap" became a key theme in John F. Kennedy's 1960 campaign for the presidency, and prompted a series of crash Pentagon programs to increase the United States' nuclear capability.

Many issues . . . inflamed superpower tensions and sustained fears on both sides that the Cold War might escalate into some form of open military conflict.

A missile gap did in fact exist—but it favored the United States rather than the Soviet Union. On the basis of new satellite photography, U.S. intelligence concluded in mid 1961 that previous estimates of Soviet nuclear strength had been vastly overstated. Indeed, by the time of the missile crisis, the Soviet Union had only some twenty to forty intercontinental ballistic missiles (ICBMs), compared to over 170 U.S. long-range missiles. The disparity in strategic bombers and submarine-launched ballistic missiles (SLBMs) was even greater. In total, the United States had some three thousand nuclear warheads ready to fire, compared to about 250 on the Soviet side.

The Kennedy administration showed no hesitation in exploiting this advantage. U.S. officials underscored America's nuclear prowess both in public speeches and in private meetings with Soviet representatives. As the disparity in power continued to widen, Soviet leaders no doubt feared that the United States might gain the ability for a preemptive nuclear strike or use its nuclear superiority to compel political concessions from the Soviets on major international disputes such as Berlin.

Berlin and the Jupiters in Turkey

The military, ideological, and geopolitical struggle between East and West converged in Berlin. Since the end of World War II, Berlin had existed as a single city, with British, French, American, and Soviet troops controlling different sectors. The presence of an armed Western enclave in the midst of communist East Germany was, as Khrushchev complained, a "bone in the throat" of Soviet leaders. In 1958, Khrushchev threatened to expel the Western powers and make Berlin a "free city" under exclusive Soviet control. Before, during, and even after August 1961, when the East Germans closed the border and constructed the infamous wall between the east and west sides of the city, Berlin's status continued to threaten a major U.S.-Soviet crisis. As Kennedy prepared for his first superpower summit in the summer of 1961, U.S. Ambassador to Moscow Llewllyn Thompson cabled Washington that Khrushchev had "so deeply committed his personal prestige and that of the Soviet Union to some action on Berlin and German problems that if we take [a] completely negative stand [on] Berlin, this would probably lead to developments in which [the] chances of war or ignominious western retreat are close to 50-50."

Disagreement over Berlin dominated the summit, which was held in Vienna on June 3 and 4, 1961. At the final session, Khrushchev informed Kennedy that the United States had until December to accept Soviet demands on Berlin, to which Kennedy replied that "it would be a cold winter." After the meeting, the president gravely told reporters that the prospect of war was now "very real."

At Vienna, Kennedy and Khrushchev also discussed other world issues, including their divergent views on, and policies toward, revolution in the Third World. Their conversation regarding Cuba foreshadowed the coming missile crisis. President Kennedy told Khrushchev that his authorization of the Bay of Pigs invasion was "a misjudgment," and that such misjudgments in the nuclear era should be avoided. According to a memorandum of the conversation, Kennedy "emphasized that the purpose of this meeting was to introduce greater precision in these judgments so that our two countries could survive this period of competition without endangering their national security." Khrushchev agreed, but he nevertheless took the opportunity to berate Kennedy for trying to overthrow Castro. If Washington believed it had the right to intervene in Cuba because Castro followed a Soviet line, Khrushchev argued, "what about Turkey and Iran?"

> These two countries are U.S. followers, they march in its wake, and they have U.S. bases and rockets. If the U.S. believes that it is free to act, then what should the USSR do? The U.S. has set a precedent for intervention in internal affairs of other countries. The USSR is

stronger than Turkey and Iran, just as the U.S. is
stronger than Cuba. This situation may cause miscalculation, to use the President's term.

As Khrushchev's remarks attest, the presence of U.S. nuclear installations and military bases close to, and even along
the borders of, the Soviet Union clearly galled Soviet leaders and was an object of extreme resentment in Moscow's
relations with the United States. As a result of NATO
agreements signed in 1959, the United States had deployed
some thirty Jupiter IRBMs [intermediate-range ballistic
missiles] in Italy and fifteen in Turkey. Even as the Jupiters
were being installed, however, U.S. analysts had concluded
that the liquid-fueled weapons were technologically obsolete; and early in his administration Kennedy began to consider the pros and cons of canceling their deployment. A
memorandum on "Turkish IRBM's," indicates, exploration
of this possibility was met coolly by Turkish (as well as Ital-
ian) officials.

---

*The United States had an established history of
invading Cuba . . . the tropical island had been
an object of empire for the United States.*

According to recent Soviet accounts, the Jupiters in
Turkey provided both an impetus and a justification for
Khrushchev's decision to deploy missiles in Cuba. Khrushchev's initial conversation with defense minister Rodion
Malinovsky took place at a retreat in the Crimea, overlook-
ing the Black Sea, at about the same time that the Jupiter
missiles in Turkey became operational. Malinovsky called
the premier's attention to the U.S. missiles just over the
horizon in Turkey and informed him that they could strike
the Soviet Union in ten minutes. As Raymond Garthoff re-
lates the story, "Khrushchev then mused on whether the Soviet Union shouldn't do the same thing in Cuba, just over
the horizon from the United States."

By that time Cuba had become the Soviet Union's first
major ally in the western hemisphere. The expansion of their
political, economic, and military relationship paralleled
mounting U.S. hostility toward Castro's regime; the more the
U.S. tried to roll back the Cuban revolution, the more the

Cubans turned to the Soviet Union for support, including weapons to defend Cuba against a potential U.S. invasion.

Most Western analysts have argued that Khrushchev and his aides decided to deploy the missiles in order to off-set the U.S. strategic advantage. But several Soviets close to the decision-making circle have recently suggested that the decision was driven in part, if not predominantly, by the desire to prevent an expected U.S. attack on Cuba. When Khrushchev discussed sending nuclear missiles to Cuba with First Deputy Prime Minister Anastas Mikoyan and then with a select group of advisers at the end of April 1962, according to Mikoyan's son, Sergo, "the main idea was the defense of Fidel":

> Khrushchev had some reasons to think the United States would repeat the Bay of Pigs, but not make mistakes anymore. . . . In 1962, at Punta del Este, Cuba was excluded from the Organization of American States. Khrushchev regarded this exclusion as a diplomatic isolation and a preparation for an invasion. And then the propagandistic preparation was the accusation of exporting revolution. So he thought an invasion was inevitable, that it would be massive, and that it would use all American force.

In early May, yet another meeting took place, this one attended by Alexandr Alekseyev, a Soviet diplomat close to Fidel Castro. According to Alekseyev's account, Khrushchev offered two rationales for sending the missiles: first, he favored deployment "to repay the Americans in kind" for encircling the Soviet Union with nuclear weapons; and second, Khrushchev saw the missiles as an "effective means of deterrence" for the inevitable U.S. invasion of Cuba.

The United States and Cuba

The United States had an established history of invading Cuba: U.S. Marines landed on Cuban shores in 1898, 1906, 1912, and 1917. Dating all the way back to the 1820s when John Quincy Adams declared that Cuba had "an importance in the sum of our national interests, with which that of no other foreign territory can be compared," the tropical island had been an object of empire for the United States. In 1859, Congress considered legislation to annex the island as a potential slave state. In 1898, the United States helped to liberate Cuba from Spanish colonial rule, only to assert aggressively its own dominion over Cuba's internal political and economic affairs. The island became known as "the pearl of the Antilles," a favorite spot for American tourists, U.S. corporations, and the mafia—with social stability maintained, between 1933 and 1958, by the corrupt pro-American military government of Fulgencio Batista. For most of his reign, General Batista could count on U.S. support and largess. Washington withdrew its military assistance just before the revolution led by Fidel Castro came to fruition in January 1959.

Washington's efforts to undermine Castro's nationalist revolution began well before his government turned hostile toward U.S. corporate holdings and then established diplomatic relations with the Soviet Union in May of 1960. Less than three months after the January 1959 revolution, President Eisenhower's National Security Council first evaluated the prospects of bringing "another government to power in Cuba." A few weeks later, in April 1959, Vice President Nixon met with Castro and immediately became, in his own words, "the strongest and most persistent advocate for setting up and supporting" covert operations to overthrow the revolutionary leader.

The CIA initiated planning for such operations in January 1960, and, by the time John F. Kennedy was elected, had already recruited and trained hundreds of Cuban exiles for a major invasion of the island. President-elect Kennedy was informed of the plan on November 18, 1960; he received a full briefing after his inauguration, and subsequently agreed to let the operation go forward with the proviso that the CIA should come up with "a quiet landing . . . without the appearance of a WW II type amphibious assault," in order to preserve the plausible denial of U.S. participation in the operation. Under no circumstances did he want to commit U.S. military personnel to a war in Cuba: "I'm not going to risk an American Hungary," he told aides. When the U.S.-sponsored landing faltered on April 16, 1962, Kennedy refused to authorize U.S. air cover—which could not have been plausibly denied—for the exile force trapped by Castro's army at Playa Girón. The result was the U.S. foreign policy disaster known as the Bay of Pigs.

Although chastened by the Bay of Pigs—"How could I have been so stupid?" Kennedy remarked to his speechwriter, Theodore Sorensen—with its failure the president and his advisers became all the more obsessed with over-throwing Castro. "We were hysterical about Castro at the time of the Bay of Pigs and thereafter," former Secretary of Defense Robert McNamara later told Senate investigators. For U.S. officials, the Cuban leader—now an avowed Marx-ist—embodied a variety of national security challenges. A week after the debacle, Walt Rostow outlined "five threats to us represented by the Castro regime": the possibility that the Soviet Union would establish an offensive air or missile base; an ideology that constituted "a moral and political of-fense to us"; Cuba's conventional arms buildup and its threat to other Latin American nations; revolutionary sub-version; and the threat of Cuba as a successful revolutionary model. A presidential task force, headed by Assistant Secre-tary of Defense Paul Nitze, similarly highlighted Castro's threat as a revolutionary example:

> He has provided a working example of a communist state in the Americas, successfully defying the United States. Thus he has appealed to widespread anti-American feeling, a feeling often shared by non-communists. His survival, in the face of persistent U.S. efforts to unseat him, has unquestionably lowered the prestige of the United States. . . . As long as Castro thrives, his major threat—the example and stimulus of a working communist revolution—will persist.

Operation Mongoose

On November 30, 1961, President Kennedy authorized a covert program known as OPERATION MONGOOSE to "use our available assets . . . to help Cuba overthrow the Communist regime." The CIA program subsequently developed under MONGOOSE would become the largest ever undertaken by the agency, involving some four hundred agents, a budget of $50 million and a variety of covert, economic, and psycho-logical operations—including assassination attempts against Fidel Castro. After the Bay of Pigs debacle, rather than turn the operation to oust Castro over to the CIA, which the pres-ident had come to distrust, oversight was given to the so-called Special Group of covert operations overseers, "aug-mented" by Attorney General Robert Kennedy and General Maxwell Taylor. According to a declassified document, a summary of the attorney general's meeting with the members of the Special Group Augmented (SGA) on December 1, he told them that a "higher authority"—that is, the president—had decided that "higher priority should be given to Cuba." The military's foremost specialist in counterinsurgency, Brigadier General Edward Lansdale, would be designated as "Chief of Operations" and tasked with fomenting "eventual revolution within Cuba."

On January 18, 1962, General Lansdale laid out the scope of "the Cuba Project." The objective would be "to help the Cubans overthrow the Communist regime from within Cuba and institute a new government with which the United States can live in peace." The coordinated means to accomplish that goal included hostile diplomacy, economic warfare, paramilitary sabotage activities, and the creation of cells of Cuban "political action agents" who could organize an internal revolt in the midst of economic and social upheaval fostered by the MONGOOSE operations. Once the anticommunist insurrection began, it was to be aided by direct U.S. military intervention. "The United States . . . will then give open support to the Cuban peoples' revolt," stated Lansdale's program review. "Such support will include military force, as necessary."

Throughout the spring of 1962, planning for overthrowing Castro became more refined. In February, Lansdale laid out a six-phase "specific plan" for the covert war to come to fruition. A declassified document reveals that intelligence, political, economic, psychological, sabotage, and military operations were supposed to culminate in an internal anti-Castro revolt in October 1962—ironically the same month the missile crisis took place—and result in a new, pro-American government by the end of that month. In his report to the SGA, Lansdale urged that the "vital decision" be made "on the use of open U.S. force to aid the Cuban people in winning their liberty." In March, the "Guidelines for OPERATION MONGOOSE" acknowledged that "final success will require decisive U.S. military intervention," but the SGA deferred that decision, limiting its authorization to intelligence work and sabotage operations. While the Pentagon prepared contingency plans for such intervention, MONGOOSE operations concentrated on acquiring intelligence in Cuba and conducting political, economic, and covert operations that would set the stage for a counterrevolution.

Phase One of operations took place between March and July 1962. During those months, the CIA acquired "hard intelligence" and established the Caribbean Admission Center at Opa-Locka, Florida, to train recruited exiles for operations inside Cuba. By the end of July, Lansdale wrote in his review of operations, the CIA would have infiltrated eleven teams and "guerrilla warfare could be activated with a good chance of success, if assisted properly." While sabotage had been planned, however, none had taken place.

Lansdale also reported that the objective of "intervention planning" had been met "fully." As part of OPERATION MONGOOSE, Pentagon strategists drafted several contingency plans for an invasion and military occupation. Throughout the spring, summer, and fall of 1962, the U.S. military conducted a series of highly visible and intimidating military exercises simulating an invasion of Cuba. In April, the military conducted LANTPHIBEX 1-62, a mock assault on the Puerto Rican island of Vieques. From April through May, the U.S. Navy carried out OPERATION QUICK KICK—maneuvers involving seventy-nine ships and forty thousand troops off the southeastern coast of the United States. SWIFT STRIKE II was conducted in August in the Carolinas. Also in August, the Defense Department announced plans for PHILBRIGLEX-62, which involved another mock military assault on the island of Vieques and the simulated overthrow of a leader named "Ortsac"—Castro spelled backward.

Psy-War Operations

Preparations for PHILBRIGLEX corresponded to a significant escalation of covert sabotage and psychological operations under OPERATION MONGOOSE. As early as February 1962, according to a previously unknown secret Pentagon memorandum for Lansdale titled "Ideas in Support of Project," the Joint Chiefs had proposed a set of psy-war options which ranged from the bizarre to the dangerous. "Operation Good Times," for example, called for distributing fake photos of "an obese Castro with two beauties . . . within a room in the Castro residence, lavishly furnished, and a table brimming over with the most delectable Cuban food with an underlying caption such as 'My ration is different.'" The falsified photo would be dropped by air over the urban centers and countryside. According to military planners, it would "put even a Commie Dictator in the proper perspective with the underprivileged masses."

A far more insidious proposal, "Operation Bingo," suggested simulating a Cuban attack on Guantanamo Base using a device called a SNAKE. The device would be placed along the perimeter of the base, and activated to simulate a firefight. Claiming that Castro's forces were trying to overrun the base, the President would then order an invasion of Cuba. "Properly executed, the above could overthrow the Cuban Government in a matter of hours," according to the Pentagon plan.

In early October, as Soviet construction of the missile sites continued unbeknownst to U.S. officials, President Kennedy brought pressure on the SGA to step up Phase Two of MONGOOSE with "more dynamic action." On October 11, Lansdale recommended a series of new action proposals, "with sabotage given priority attention." These operations included actions to bomb and "destroy" Cuban-owned ships, and a Voice of America Russian propaganda program aimed at inciting hostilities between Soviet technicians in Cuba and the Cuban public. At a planning meeting held on October 14, just one day before the missiles were discovered, the SGA agreed that "all efforts should be made to develop new and imaginative approaches with the possibility of getting rid of the Castro regime."

Even after the missile crisis began, the President and his brother pushed for more action. Indeed, Robert Kennedy went from the first meeting of the EXCOMM on the morning of October 16, to a 2 P.M. meeting with MONGOOSE officials where he expressed the "general dissatisfaction of the President" with the lack of progress on sabotage. The CIA and others, according to the Attorney General, had shown "no push" for concrete acts, and he made a plea for "new ideas of things that could be done against Cuba." In an oblique reference to the missile crisis—which a number of those in the room did not yet know about—Kennedy noted a "change in atmosphere" over the last twenty-four hours, and asked for intelligence on how many Cubans would defend Castro's government if the United States invaded Cuba.

From the Soviet and Cuban perspective, the military maneuvers and covert operations, combined with the implementation of a full economic embargo in February 1962 and a U.S.-led diplomatic initiative to expel Cuba from the

Organization of American States and isolate Castro, added up to preparations for an invasion. Cuban intelligence had infiltrated exile groups recruited for MONGOOSE and, according to Kennedy's press secretary, Pierre Salinger, had obtained internal memoranda that discussed the timetable for an invasion. Former Kennedy administration officials have since stated categorically, and repeatedly, that while there were contingency plans, at no time following the Bay of Pigs had the president authorized an invasion. The Soviet-Cuban perception was, however, understandable. "I state quite frankly," former secretary of defense Robert McNamara declared at the Havana conference, "that if I had been a Cuban leader at that time, I might well have concluded that there was a great risk of U.S. invasion. And I should say, as well, if I had been a Soviet leader at the time, I might have come to the same conclusion."

In preparation for that invasion, high-level Soviet and Cuban officials secretly negotiated the deployment of the missiles, as well as vast amounts of other military armaments and a large contingent of conventionally armed Soviet troops. In July, Raúl Castro traveled to Moscow and, with Marshal Malinovsky, drew up and initialed a draft military cooperation agreement to take the necessary steps "to jointly defend [the] legitimate rights of the people of Cuba . . . in the face of possible aggression." Che Guevara carried a revised draft back to Moscow at the end of August. Although Khrushchev never signed the pact, by midsummer the Soviets had begun the transfer of advanced air defense equipment, MiG-21 interceptors, coastal defense forces, and combat personnel eventually totalling forty-two thousand troops.

Kennedy administration officials and the intelligence community monitored this massive deployment with growing concern. On August 22, the CIA released an intelligence assessment on "Recent Soviet Military Aid to Cuba." The study cited an "unprecedented" level of military activities and observed that "clearly something new and different is taking place." A CIA National Intelligence Estimate (NIE), dated in mid September, noted the possibility that the Soviets were moving nuclear arms into Cuba. Nonetheless, the NIE concluded that the deployment of nuclear missiles "would be incompatible with Soviet practice to date and with Soviet policy as we presently estimate it."

Unconvinced that the Soviets would deploy nuclear missiles, but alarmed enough to prepare for that contingency, President Kennedy's National Security Advisor McGeorge Bundy issued National Security Memorandum 181 on August 23. The presidential directive called for upgrading analysis of Soviet shipments, military contingency planning for eliminating nuclear installations in Cuba, development "with all possible speed" of new OPERATION MONGOOSE activities and, presciently, an assessment of actions "to get Jupiter missiles out of Turkey." Kennedy's advisers also recommended that he publicly "draw the line," as Walt Rostow suggested on September 3, "at the installation in Cuba or in Cuban waters of nuclear weapons or delivery vehicles, sea or land based."

On September 4, President Kennedy issued a public statement to address a growing cacophony of rumors and allegations on Capitol Hill. There was no evidence of "offensive ground-to-ground missiles" in Cuba, he stated. "Were it to be otherwise, the gravest issues would arise." Even as Soviet diplomats assured U.S. officials that all weapons going to Cuba were defensive, Kennedy reiterated the U.S. position again during a press conference on September 13. If Cuba should ever "become an offensive military base of significant capacity for the Soviet Union," he declared, the United States would "do whatever must be done to protect its own security. . . ."

2

The Soviet Union Deployed the Missiles to Defend Cuba

Nikita Khrushchev

Soviet premier Nikita Khrushchev traces how the relations between the Soviet Union and Cuba evolved, how the Soviet Union supplied military and economic help to the fledgling Communist state, the U.S. campaign to destabilize Castro, and finally, how the leaders of the two countries decided to deploy the missiles in Cuba. Khrushchev, a reformist, predated Mikhail Gorbachev in initiating changes in the Soviet system through his "de-Stalinization" campaign. He led the Soviet Union from 1953 to 1964. Many scholars claim Communist hardliners eased him out because of his handling of the missile crisis. He died in 1971.

Cuba's geographical position has always made it very vulnerable to its enemies. The Cuban coast is only a few miles from the American shore, and it is stretched out like a sausage, a shape that makes it easy for attackers and incredibly difficult for the island's defenders. There are infinite opportunities for invasion, especially if the invader has naval artillery and air support.

We were sure that the Americans would never reconcile themselves to the existence of Castro's Cuba. They feared, as much as we hoped, that a Socialist Cuba might become a magnet that would attract other Latin American countries to Socialism. Given the continual threat of American interference in the Caribbean, what should our own policy be? This question was constantly on my mind, and I frequently discussed it with the other members of the Presidium. Everyone agreed that America would not leave Cuba alone unless we did something. We had an obligation to do everything in our power to protect Cuba's existence as a Socialist country and as a working example to the other countries of Latin America. It was clear to me that we might very well lose Cuba if we didn't take some decisive steps in her defense.

The fate of Cuba and the maintenance of Soviet prestige in that part of the world preoccupied me even when I was busy conducting the affairs of state in Moscow and traveling to the other fraternal countries. While I was on an official visit to Bulgaria, for instance, one thought kept hammering away at my brain: what will happen if we lose Cuba? I knew it would have been a terrible blow to Marxism-Leninism. It would gravely diminish our stature throughout the would, but especially in Latin America. If Cuba fell, other Latin American countries would reject us, claiming that for all our might the Soviet Union hadn't been able to do anything for Cuba except to make empty protests to the United Nations. We had to think up some way of confronting America with more than words. We had to establish a tangible and effective deterrent to American interference in the Caribbean. But what exactly? The logical answer was missiles. The United States had already surrounded the Soviet Union with its own bomber bases and missiles. We knew that American missiles were aimed against us in Turkey and Italy, to say nothing of West Germany. Our vital industrial centers were directly threatened by planes armed with atomic bombs and guided missiles tipped with nuclear warheads. As Chairman of the Council of Ministers, I found myself in the difficult position of having to decide on a course of action which would answer the American threat but which would also avoid war. Any fool can start a war, and once he's done so, even the wisest of men are helpless to stop it—especially if it's a nuclear war.

It was during my visit to Bulgaria that I had the idea of installing missiles with nuclear warheads in Cuba without letting the United States find out they were there until it was too late to do anything about them. I knew that first we'd have to talk to Castro and explain our strategy to him in order to get the agreement of the Cuban government.

My thinking went like this: if we installed the missiles secretly and then if the United States discovered the missiles were there after they were already poised and ready to strike, the Americans would think twice before trying to liquidate our installations by military means. I knew that the United States could knock out some of our installations, but not all of them. If a quarter or even a tenth of our missiles survived—even if only one or two big ones were left—we could still hit New York, and there wouldn't be much of New York left. I don't mean to say that everyone in New York would be killed—not everyone, of course, but an awful lot of people would be wiped out. I don't know how many: that's a matter for our scientists and military personnel to work out. They specialize in nuclear warfare and know how to calculate the consequences of a missile strike against a city the size of New York. But that's all beside the point. The main thing was that the installation of our missiles in Cuba would, I thought, restrain the United States from precipitous military action against Castro's government. In addition to protecting Cuba, our missiles would have equalized what the West likes to call "the balance of power." The Americans had surrounded our country with military bases and threatened us with nuclear weapons, and now they would learn just what it feels like to have enemy missiles pointing at you; we'd be doing nothing more than giving them a little of their own medicine. And it was high time America learned what it feels like to have her own land and her own people threatened. . . .

No Desire to Start a War

In the course of discussions inside the Government, we decided to install intermediate-range missiles, launching equipment, and Il-28 bombers in Cuba. Even though these bombers were obsolete, they would be useful against an enemy landing force. The Il-28 was too slow to fly over enemy territory because it could easily be shot down, but was well suited for coastal defense. The Il-28 was our first jet bomber. In its time it had been god of the air, but by the time we gave military assistance to Cuba, the Il-28 had already been taken out of production.

Soon after we began shipping our missiles to Cuba, the Americans became suspicious. Their intelligence told them that the number of our ships going to Cuba had suddenly and substantially increased and that our own people were unloading the ships once they reached Cuban ports. We didn't allow the Cubans to do any of the unloading or installation of the missiles themselves. While the Americans had no direct information about what we were delivering, they knew that whatever we were doing, we were doing with our own hands. It was not long before they concluded on the basis of reconnaissance photographs that we were installing missiles. They also knew about our Il-28 bombers which had been flown to Cuba.

The Americans became frightened, and we stepped up our shipments. We had delivered almost everything by the time the crisis reached the boiling point.

There are people who argue with the benefit of hindsight that antiaircraft missiles should have been installed before the ballistic missiles so as to close the airspace over Cuba. This doesn't make sense. How many surface-to-air missiles can you fit on a tiny sausage-shaped island? There's a limit to the number of missile installations you can put on an island as small as Cuba. Then, after you've launched all your missiles, you're completely unprotected. Moreover, antiaircraft missiles have a very short range. Antiaircraft batteries can easily be knocked out from the sea and air.

The combination of the location of Cuba and the power of the Soviet Union was very threatening to the United States.

I want to make one thing absolutely clear: when we put our ballistic missiles in Cuba, we had no desire to start a war. On the contrary, our principal aim was only to deter America from starting a war. We were well aware that a war which started over Cuba would quickly expand into a world war. Any idiot could have started a war between America and Cuba. Cuba was eleven thousand kilometers away from us. Only a fool would think that we wanted to invade the American continent from Cuba. Our goal was precisely the opposite: we wanted to keep the Americans from invading Cuba, and, to that end, we wanted to make them think twice by confronting them with our missiles. This goal we achieved— but not without undergoing a period of perilous tension.

A Dose of Their Own Medicine

When the Americans figured out what we were up to in Cuba, they mounted a huge press campaign against us, claiming that we were threatening the security of the United States and so on and so forth. In short, hostility began to build up, and the American press fanned the flames. Then one day in October President Kennedy came out with a statement warning that the United States would take whatever measures were necessary to remove what he called the "threat" of Russian missiles on Cuba. The Americans began to make a belligerent show of their strength. They concentrated their forces against Cuba, completely surrounding the island with their navy. Things started churning. In our estimation the Americans were trying to frighten us, but they were no less scared than we were of atomic war. We hadn't had time to deliver all our shipments to Cuba, but we had installed enough missiles already to destroy New York, Chicago, and the other huge industrial cities, not to mention a little village like Washington. I don't think America had ever faced such a real threat of destruction as at that moment.

Meanwhile we went about our own business. We didn't let ourselves be intimidated. Our ships, with the remainder of our deliveries to Cuba, headed straight through an armada of the American navy, but the Americans didn't try to stop our ships or even check them. We kept in mind that as long as the United States limited itself to threatening gestures and didn't actually touch us, we could afford to pretend to ignore the harassment. After all, the United States had no moral or legal quarrel with us. We hadn't given the Cubans anything more than the Americans were giving to their allies. We had the same rights and opportunities as the Americans. Our conduct in the international arena was governed by the same rules and limits as the Americans'.

We had almost completed our shipments. As the crisis approached the boiling point, the Western press began to seethe with anger and alarm. We replied accordingly, although not so hysterically. Our people were fully informed of the dangerous situation that had developed, although we took care not to cause panic by the way we presented the facts. . . .

We had to establish a tangible and effective deterrent to American interference in the Caribbean. . . . The logical answer was missiles.

Then the exchange of notes began. I dictated the messages and conducted the exchange from our side. I spent one of the most dangerous nights at the Council of Ministers office in the Kremlin. I slept on a couch in my office— and I kept my clothes on. I didn't want to be like that Western minister who was caught literally with his pants down by the Suez events of 1956 and who had to run around in his shorts until the emergency was over. I was ready for alarming news to come any moment, and I wanted to be ready to react immediately.

President Kennedy issued an ultimatum, demanding that we remove our missiles and bombers from Cuba. I remember those days vividly. I remember the exchange with President Kennedy especially well because I initiated it and was at the center of the action on our end of the correspondence. I take complete responsibility for the fact that the President and I entered into direct contact at the most crucial and dangerous stage of the crisis.

The climax came after five or six days, when our ambassador to Washington, Anatoly Dobrynin, reported that the President's brother, Robert Kennedy, had come to see him on an unofficial visit. Dobrynin's report went something like this:

> Robert Kennedy looked exhausted. One could see from his eyes that he had not slept for days. He himself

said that he had not been home for six days and nights. 'The President is in a grave situation,' Robert Kennedy said, 'and he does not know how to get out of it. We are under very severe stress. In fact we are under pressure from our military to use force against Cuba. Probably at this very moment the President is sitting down to write a message to Chairman Khrushchev. We want to ask you, Mr. Dobrynin, to pass President Kennedy's message to Chairman Khrushchev through unofficial channels. President Kennedy implores Chairman Khrushchev to accept his offer and to take into consideration the peculiarities of the American system. Even though the President himself is very much against starting a war over Cuba, an irreversible chain of events could occur against his will. That is why the President is appealing directly to Chairman Khrushchev for his help in liquidating this conflict. If the situation continues much longer, the President is not sure that the military will not overthrow him and seize power. The American army could get out of control.'

Withdrawal After a Pledge of Non-Invasion

I hadn't overlooked this possibility. We knew that Kennedy was a young President and that the security of the United States was indeed threatened. For some time we had felt there was a danger that the President would lose control of his military, and now he was admitting this to us himself. Kennedy's message urgently repeated the Americans' demand that we remove the missiles and bombers from Cuba. We could sense from the tone of the message that tension in the United States was indeed reaching a critical point.

We wrote a reply to Kennedy in which we said that we had installed the missiles with the goal of defending Cuba and that we were not pursuing any other aims except to deter an invasion of Cuba and to guarantee that Cuba could follow a course determined by its own people rather than one dictated by some third party.

While we conducted some of this exchange through official diplomatic channels, the more confidential letters were relayed to us through the President's brother. He gave Dobrynin his telephone number and asked him to call at any time. Once, when Robert Kennedy talked with Dobrynin, he was almost crying. "I haven't seen my children for days now," Robert Kennedy said, "and the President hasn't seen his either. We're spending all day and night at the White House; I don't know how much longer we can hold out against our generals." . . .

I should mention that our side's policy was, from the outset, worked out in the collective leadership. It wasn't until after two or three lengthy discussions of the matter that we had decided it was worth the risk to install missiles on Cuba in the first place. It had been my feeling that the initial, as well as the subsequent, decisions should not be forced down anyone's throat. I had made sure to give the collective leadership time for the problem to crystallize in everyone's mind. I had wanted my comrades to accept and support the decision with a clear conscience and a full understanding of what the consequences of putting the missiles on Cuba might be—namely, war with the United States. Every step we had taken had been carefully considered by the collective.

As soon as we announced publicly that we were ready to remove our missiles from Cuba, the Americans became arrogant and insisted on sending an inspection team to the island. We answered that they'd have to get the Cuban government's permission to do that. Then the Chinese and American press started hooting and shouting about how Khrushchev had turned coward and backed down. I won't deny that we were obliged to make some big concessions in the interests of peace. We even consented to the inspection of our ships—but only from the air. We never let the Americans actually set foot on our decks, though we did let them satisfy themselves that we were really removing our missiles.

When we put our ballistic missiles in Cuba, we had no desire to start a war . . . our principal aim was only to deter America from starting a war.

Once the evacuation was begun, there was some question in our minds whether the Americans would pull back their naval forces which surrounded the island. We were worried that as soon as we retreated the Americans might move in on the offensive. But no, good sense prevailed. Their ships started to leave Cuba's territorial waters, but their planes continued to circle the island. Castro gave an order to open fire, and the Cubans shot down an American U-2 reconnaissance plane. Thus another American spy, just like Gary Powers, was downed by one of our missiles. The incident caused an uproar. At first we were concerned that President Kennedy wouldn't be able to stomach the humiliation. Fortunately, however, nothing happened except that the Americans became more brazen than ever in their propaganda. They did everything they could to wound our pride and to make Kennedy look good. But that didn't matter as long as they pulled back their troops and called off their air force.

[Kennedy] . . . was gifted with the ability to resolve international conflicts by negotiation, as the whole world learned during the so-called Cuban crisis.

The situation was stabilizing. Almost immediately after the President and I had exchanged notes at the peak of the crisis, our relations with the United States started to return to normal. Our relations with Cuba, on the other hand, took a sudden turn for the worse. Castro even stopped receiving our ambassador. It seemed that by removing our missiles we had suffered a moral defeat in the eyes of the Cubans. Our shares in Cuba instead of going up, went down. . . .

A Compromise Was Found

In our negotiations with the Americans during the crisis, they had, on the whole, been open and candid with us, especially Robert Kennedy. The Americans knew that if Russian blood were shed in Cuba, American blood would surely be shed in Germany. The American government was anxious to avoid such a development. It had been, to say the least, an interesting and challenging situation. The two most powerful nations of the world had been squared off against each other, each with its finger on the button. You'd have thought that war was inevitable. But both sides showed that if the desire to avoid war is strong enough, even the most pressing dispute can be solved by compromise. And a compromise over Cuba was indeed found. The episode ended in a triumph of common sense. I'll always remember the late President with deep respect because, in the final analysis, he showed himself to be sober-minded and determined to avoid war. He didn't let himself become frightened, nor did he become reckless. He didn't overestimate America's might, and he left himself a way out of the crisis. He showed real wisdom and statesmanship when he turned his back on right-wing forces in the United States who were trying to goad him into taking military action against Cuba. It was a great victory for us, though, that we had been able to extract from Kennedy a promise that neither America nor any of her allies would invade Cuba. . . .

A number of years have passed, and we can be gratified that the revolutionary government of Fidel Castro still lives and grows. So far, the United States has abided by its promise not to interfere in Cuba nor to let anyone else interfere. . . .

Today Cuba exists as an independent Socialist country, right in front of the open jaws of predatory American imperialism. Cuba's very existence is good propaganda for other Latin American countries, encouraging them to follow its example and to choose the course of Socialism. Other Latin American peoples are already beginning to realize what steps they can take to liberate themselves from American imperialists and monopolists. Hopefully Cuba's example will continue to shine.

As for Kennedy, his death was a great loss. He was gifted with the ability to resolve international conflicts by negotiation, as the whole world learned during the so-called Cuban crisis. Regardless of his youth he was a real statesman. I believe that if Kennedy had lived, relations between the Soviet Union and the United States would be much better than they are. Why do I say that? Because Kennedy would have never let his country get bogged down in Vietnam.

After President Kennedy's death, his successor, Lyndon Johnson, assured us that he would keep Kennedy's promise not to invade Cuba. So far the Americans have not broken their word. If they ever do, we still have the means necessary to make good on our own commitment to Castro and to defend Cuba.

3

Cuba Accepted the Missiles to Defend Socialism

Fidel Castro

Cuban leader Fidel Castro traces the cause of the missile crisis to U.S. efforts to sabotage Cuba, particularly the Bay of Pigs, the failed U.S. invasion plan of 1961. He asserts that Cuba has the right to arm itself with weapons it deems necessary in defending itself. Fidel Castro led his country in overthrowing the dictatorship of Fulgencio Batista and in installing a Socialist state in 1959. After turning Communist and aligning with the Soviet Union, he became the nemesis of the United States. Today, Castro continues to lead Cuba, while the U.S. continues its policy of economic embargo against the Caribbean nation.

First of all, when the issue of the missiles was first brought up, we thought that it was something beneficial to the consolidation of the defensive power of the entire socialist bloc, that it would contribute to this. We did not want to concentrate on our problems. Subsequently, it represented our defense. Subsequently. But really, the comrades who participated were the comrades of the directorate, who met to analyze this problem and make a decision. And how was it presented: That in our opinion it would strengthen the socialist bloc.

If we held the belief that the socialist bloc should be willing to go to war for the sake of any other socialist country, we did not have any right to consider something that

Excerpted from Fidel Castro's remarks at the Havana conference on the Cuban Missile Crisis, February 28, 1992.

could represent a danger to us. The questions of propaganda stayed within us, but we also saw the real danger of any crisis that could emerge, but without any hesitation, and honestly, thinking in a truly internationalist manner. All the comrades decided to give an immediate response. Keeping in mind the affirmative answer—with an enormous trust in a country that we believed was experienced in many things, even in war, and in international affairs—we told, we stated to them the usefulness of signing a military accord. Then, they sent an accord bill. . . .

Here I have what I said, textually, in a private conversation in 1968, regarding the antecedents of the October Crisis. In all truth and summarizing, we, from the beginning, saw it as a strategic operation. I am going to tell the truth about how we thought. We did not like the missiles. If it was a matter of our defense alone, we would not have accepted the missiles here. But, do not think that it was because of the dangers that could come from having the missiles here, but rather because of the way in which this could damage the image of the revolution. We were very committed to the image of the revolution in the rest of Latin America.

If it was to strengthen the socialist bloc . . . and if it would contribute to Cuba's defense, we were willing to receive all the missiles that might be needed.

The fact that the presence of the missiles would turn us into a Soviet military base would have a high political cost for our country's image, which we valued so highly. So if it had been for our defense—and I say this here with all honesty. Aleksandr [Alekseyev] knows this—we would not have accepted the missiles. But we really saw in the issue of the missile installation something that would strengthen the socialist bloc, something that would help in some way to improve the so-called correlation of forces. That was how we perceived it immediately, immediately, instantaneously.

We did not argue about this. It would not have made sense, because if we had argued about what they were for, in fact, the conclusion we would draw would be that they should not be brought. In fact, we would have refused to accept the missiles because, of course, their presence was not presented in those terms. That was what we perceived immediately. Then we asked a few questions about what kind of missiles and how many. We did not have any practical knowledge about these things, and we were informed that they would deploy 42 missiles. From what has been shown here, it seems there were 36 operational missiles and six for testing. But they told us there would be 42 missiles. We asked for time because we had to meet with the leadership and to inform them about all this before coming to a decision, but we said we would do this quickly.

In fact, when this meeting was over, we organized a meeting of the leadership, and we analyzed the matter in the terms that I have explained. We said that the presence of the missiles had this and that significance. We also were not unaware—and for me it was obvious—that the presence of the missiles was going to give rise to great political tension. That was obvious. But we saw this matter from the angle of our moral, political, and internationalist duties. That was how we understood it.

There was talk about the missiles in a different sense. After the Bay of Pigs invasion, there had already been talk about missiles. You would have to review all of Nikita's statements. He insinuated more than once that an invasion of Cuba could be responded to with the use of missiles. He insinuated this more than once, publicly, to such an extent that everyone here was talking about the Soviet missiles before the crisis, after the Bay of Pigs, as if they were their property. Many comrades talked about the missiles in their speeches. However, I refrained from saying a single word about [the] missiles, because it did not seem right to me that our people, our populace, should place their hopes for defense in support from abroad. . . .

That is why I did not talk about the Soviet missiles as a possible aid in any of my speeches, and there are quite a few in that period. Nikita encouraged this matter a lot with his public statements. As was also acknowledged . . . even in the United States, even Kennedy said in his campaign that he thought that there was an imbalance in strategic missiles. Throughout the world, people thought there was an imbalance in strategic missiles. It was known that the Americans had a very powerful air force, but that the Soviet Union had made great progress in the area of rocketry.

During those days, there were spectacular technical achievements like the space flights. The first space flight was made by a Soviet pilot, in a space capsule. All of that had an enormous effect on world opinion, and from what I can see, it also had an enormous effect in the United States. It is not at all strange that we would have more or less similar ideas about the combat capacity of each of the great powers in this area of nuclear missiles.

But everyone thought this, and assuming that the USSR had many more missiles than they had, we perceived that the presence of these missiles here in Cuba meant a modification . . . [changes thought] not a change; we cannot talk about a change in the correlation of forces, but it was a considerable improvement in the correlation of forces in favor of the socialist countries that we saw as our allies, friends, and brothers—sharing a common ideology.

For Defense, Not for Attack

Of course, we never saw the missiles as something that could one day be used against the United States, in an attack against the United States, an unjustified attack or a first strike. I remember that Nikita was always repeating; that they would never make a first strike, a nuclear strike. This issue was an obsession of his. He was constantly talking about peace. He was constantly talking about negotiations with the United States, of ending the Cold War, the arms race, etc.

So to judge the mood of that time, one should understand what was thought about this and about the strength of each of the great powers. But we saw that this improved the situation of the socialist bloc, and we really saw the issue of Cuba's defense as a secondary matter, for the reasons I have explained. So that was how we saw it, and we have continued to have this perception throughout all these years. That is why I read this speech 24 years ago. If one sees that the correlation. . . . [rephrases] Knowing what one knows now, one can see the practical military importance these rockets had, because they really turned medium-range missiles into strategic missiles.

When we returned to the meeting with the marshall and (Rachidov), we gave them our answer. . . .

If it was to strengthen the socialist bloc, and also—and I put this in second place—if it would contribute to Cuba's defense, we were willing to receive all the missiles that might be needed. To be more faithful, we said that we were willing to receive up to 1,000 missiles, if they wanted to send them. Those were our words, verbatim. I used the words: 1,000. I said: This is our resolution. . . . If the decision has already been made, it has already been made. But it was made in that spirit and with that intention. This may also explain why we felt so indignant about the later development of events, about what happened. Because we practically took an attitude of rebellion and intransigence about the crisis. . . .

Cuba's Right to Defend Itself

In public statements the [Cuban] government made and in the statements at the United Nations, we always said that Cuba considered that it had a sovereign right to have whatever kind of weapons it thought appropriate, and no one had any right to establish what kind of weapons our country could or could not have. We never went along with denying the strategic nature of the weapons. We never did. We did not agree to that game. We did not agree with that approach. Therefore, we never denied or confirmed the nature of the weapons; rather, we reaffirmed our right to have whatever type of weapons we thought appropriate for our defense.

In contrast, to tell the truth, Khrushchev went along with the game of categorizing the weapons. He turned it into something intentional. Since he did not have any intention of using the weapons in an offensive operation, he believed that it was the intention that defined the nature of the weapons. But it was very clear that Kennedy did not understand it that way. Kennedy did not understand the issue of intentions but rather the issue of type of weapons, whether they were strategic weapons or not. That was the issue. It can be seen very clearly that Kennedy was convinced that strategic weapons were not going to be brought to Cuba.

Because of this, I would say that there was something more than shrewdness here. Deception was involved here. I think the two things—the secrecy about the military agreement and the deception—were two facts, two facts that did harm. Because I think a different approach should have been adopted, and not the approach of deceit. . . .

So, in my opinion, Kennedy trusted in what he was told.

This is seen in all his public statements. It was like a relief to him to think: Well, they are filling that country with tanks or cannons or who knows what, but there are no strategic weapons there. He thought according to a rationale; he made calculations according to a rationale. This naturally gave him, not legal force, but it gave him the opportunity to present himself to world public opinion as one who had been deceived. . . .

We would not have opposed a solution . . . but it had to be an acceptable and honorable solution.

What other advantage did it give him? That when the missile sites were finally discovered on 14 October, the United States had an enormous advantage because they held the secret in their hands. They could take the initiative. The initiative in the military realm was put into the hands of the United States because they knew what was happening and could afford to choose one option or another, a political option, a quarantine, or a surprise air attack on those installations.

I think that was a very dangerous moment, from the military point of view—even if it was illegal, arbitrary, and unjust, or even immoral from any point of view because you have to comply with international laws. You do not have the right to attack any country or invade any country. But, well, he had the choice in his hands. There could have been a surprise strike when no one was expecting it. . . .

Cuba's Demands

Of course, when this news [Khrushchev's decision to withdraw the missiles] arrived, it provoked a great indignation because we realized that we had become some type of game token. We not only saw a unilateral decision; a series of steps had been taken without including us. They could have told us; there was the message on the 26th and on the 27th. There had been time, but we heard on the radio on the 28th that an agreement had taken place. We had to endure the humiliation. I understood the Soviet officer when he said that it was the most painful decision that he had to obey in his life, the issue of the inspection of the ships.

We found out about the agreement on the 28th. I believe that there was a message on the way, informing us after the fact. It arrived one or two hours later through the embassy. The reaction of all the people, of all the people, all the cadres, of all the comrades was of profound indignation, it was not a feeling of relief. Then, the political decision that we immediately took was to issue the five-point demands on that same day, the 28th. . . .

There were five points, very simple and easy to remember.

1. The end of the economic blockade and of all the economic and trade pressure measures that the United States implemented throughout the world against our country;

2. The end of all subversive actions, shipment and infiltration of weapons and explosives by air or sea, organization of mercenary invasions, infiltration of spies and saboteurs, actions that are carried out from U.S. territory and certain accomplice countries;

3. The end to all pirate attacks conducted from existing bases in the United States and in Puerto Rico;

4. The end of all violations of our airspace and waters by U.S. aircraft and warships;

5. The withdrawal from the Guantanamo Naval Base and the return of the territory occupied by the United States.

These were the five points that we issued on the 28th as our demands.

We would not have opposed a solution. If there was a real danger of war, if we would have known that Nikita was willing to withdraw the missiles and find a solution on that basis, and on a truly honorable basis, we would not have refused. Logically, there was no purpose in insisting on a situation or a solution, but it had to be an acceptable and honorable solution.

4

Cuba's Actions Affected the Outcome of the Crisis

Philip Brenner

Philip Brenner observes that most studies on the Cuban missile crisis exclude Cuba, which he believes is a mistake. He believes that the crisis' lessons can be understood more adequately if Cuba's perceptions and motivations are brought into the discussion. At the time of writing, Brenner was chairman of the Department of International Politics and Foreign Policy at the Washington University in Washington, D.C. He is the author of *From Confrontation to Negotiation: Relations with Cuba*. He has contributed to the declassification of documents on the missile crisis not only in the United States but in Russia and Cuba as well.

W hile there have been conflicting reports in the past over who initiated the plan to bring missiles to Cuba, [Prime Minister] Castro's accounts are consistent with other evidence that indicates the idea was first raised by the Soviets in May 1962. Emilio Aragones Navarro reported in 1989 that six Cuban officials were involved in the decision, and that they unanimously agreed to accept the offer: Fidel Castro, Raúl Castro, Che Guevara, Blas Roca, Osvaldo Dorticós, and Aragones. The six formed the Secretariat of the Integrated Revolutionary Organizations (ORI), the ruling party at the time.

A trip to Moscow by Raúl Castro in July served to develop details of the plan and during those two weeks a formal agreement was drafted and initialled. However, the agreement was never finalized. Fidel Castro amended the July draft, he explained in January 1992, because the initial "draft was erratic, in the sense that there was no clear foundation set about the matter." The new draft emphasized that Cuba and the Soviet Union were "guiding themselves by the principles and objectives of the United Nations Organization Charter," and were "taking into account the urgency of taking measures to assure mutual defense in the face of possible aggression against the Republic of Cuba and the [Union of Soviet Socialist Republics] USSR." The agreement did not make any mention of missiles, or any other equipment to be delivered to Cuba. . . .

To exclude Cuba from the missile crisis is akin to "saying that Hamlet *can be played without a stage."*

By the end of October there were more than 40,000 Soviet military personnel on the island, about half of whom were troops. We do not know if the Cubans requested this large number, whether they sought even more, or how they considered the troops would be used. Such a significant Soviet military contingent in itself would likely have prompted a U.S. attack, because it would have made Cuba a major Soviet base. With such a large contingent, the Soviet stakes in a U.S. attack would also have been enormous. Were the Soviet troops overrun by U.S. forces, [Soviet] Premier [Nikita] Khrushchev might not have survived the ensuing humiliation.

Che Guevara and Aragones traveled to Moscow on 27 August to finalize the missile agreement, after Castro had made amendments to the July draft. Aragones asserted in 1989 that he sought to make the agreement public immediately. The missile deployment was badly camouflaged, and there was Cuban concern as to whether the missiles could be kept secret from the United States. Cuba also reasoned that an announcement about the missiles would gain it more security than the secret installation of offensive weapons. Indeed, former White House official Theodore

Sorensen reflected at the 1989 Moscow conference that it would have been more difficult for the United States to compel withdrawal of the missiles had the agreement been made public, because then the situation would have paralleled U.S. agreements with countries on the Soviet periphery. Castro suggested a similar line of argument in 1992, when he recalled that he had opposed installing the missiles in secret. "The secrecy of the military agreement did harm," he said. There would have been significant protests against the United States for initiating a quarantine, he explained, "if we had done things openly. All of this is true because we were within our most absolute right to do so [deploy the missiles]. And how, if we had the right, were we going to act in a way that made it seem that we did not have this right, that made it seem that we were doing something wrong."

From the Cuban perspective, a public agreement in itself would have had a deterrent effect, similar to membership in the Warsaw Pact, by making an attack against Cuba equivalent to an attack against the Soviet Union. Cuba did not take Soviet protection for granted, and it sought to maneuver the Soviet Union into an embrace at the same time Cuba sought to protect itself from the United States. Such an alliance was precisely what the Soviets had resisted, because of the difficulties that would be entailed in sustaining a conflict with the United States so far from the Soviet Union. Khrushchev refused to make the agreement public, and proposed to announce the accord in November, once the missiles were operational. It was never signed formally by the Cuban or Soviet heads of state.

Cuba Played an Active Role

Journalist Herbert Matthews argues that to exclude Cuba from the missile crisis is akin to "saying that *Hamlet* can be played without a stage." The metaphor unfortunately suggests that Cuba played a passive role, that it was no more than the inanimate stage for the superpower players. While the review of the period before 22 October already has invalidated the metaphor, the notion that Cuba had little impact on events during the height of the crisis may have been the most serious oversight in earlier studies.

The response in Cuba to President Kennedy's 22 October announcement of the quarantine was apparently, in Matthews's phrasing, "a curious mixture of exhilaration and calm." As filmmaker Adolfo Gilly observed, "It was as if a long-contained tension relaxed, as if the whole country had said as one, 'at last.'" Castro himself was reportedly quite calm, perhaps because he had experienced the possibility of total defeat several times before. "For Kennedy and the United States," political scientist Herbert Dinerstein reasoned, "this was the first time."

The exhilaration undoubtedly came from the full-scale mobilization announced by Castro as President Kennedy spoke on 22 October. With a seeming certainty that the United States would launch a major invasion of the island, the official government newspaper *Revolucion* was emblazoned by a headline on 23 October that read: "The Nation on a War Footing." Sergio del Valle Jímenez, then Cuban army chief of staff, recalled in 1989 that the Cuban leaders anticipated there would be massive U.S. bombing with an invasion, and they had ordered the erection of ramparts and the digging of trenches. He said that 270,000 people were placed under arms within days. *The CINCLANT Account* reports that "Cuban Army units mobilized and assumed defensive positions quickly and with a minimum of confusion." Interestingly, it seems that there was not a roundup of suspected counterrevolutionaries and dissidents, as there had been during the Bay of Pigs invasion. This may have been due to the sense that the danger to Cuba this time was from a direct U.S. attack, not from subversive forces. . . .

Ready for War

Had the United States invaded Cuba—there are indications that an invasion was being prepared for 29 or 30 October in order to resolve the crisis—military preparations by Cuba would have made the ensuing conflict different from the one anticipated by U.S. planners. The U.S. expectation was that the main fighting would have been over in ten days, and that U.S. forces would sustain 18,484 casualties. However, in Moscow in 1989, Cuban Political Bureau member Jorge Risquet argued that major guerrilla warfare would have gone on for years, and del Valle estimated that there would have been 100,000 civilian and military casualties in the short term. More important, as indicated above, the United States was unaware that there were nine Soviet tactical nuclear missiles (*Lunas*) on the island that were armed with warheads of between 7,000 and 12,000 tons of TNT equivalent. (This was comparable to the bombs that destroyed Hiroshima and Nagasaki.) Moreover, the Soviet general in command on the island had the authority to fire these missiles in the event of a U.S. invasion. Such a nuclear strike on the 140,000 invading U.S. forces would have resulted in tens of thousands of deaths and a near certain retaliatory U.S. nuclear strike. It would have been difficult to contain the likely ensuing escalations.

The Kennedy-Khrushchev agreements had to be implemented and Cuba became very much a part of that process.

One indication of the ferocity of the Cuban position, and the willingness to throw caution to the wind, was Castro's order on 27 October to open fire on any hostile aircraft in Cuban airspace. That morning a Soviet officer, who may have been responding to Castro's general command instead of following instructions from Moscow to avoid provocations, fired a SAM that downed a U-2 surveillance aircraft. On the afternoon of the 27th, at the height of the crisis, Cuban 37 mm guns hit a low-flying F8U-1P plane that was on a reconnaissance mission. (Cuban forces controlled the island's antiaircraft batteries, which apparently became operational between 24 October and 27 October.)

Had the F8U-1P been unable to return to base, it is likely that the threatened U.S. attacks would have commenced. There already was pressure on President Kennedy from several of his advisers and from the Joint Chiefs of Staff to launch an attack, at least against the surface-to-air and ballistic missiles. With a second reconnaissance plane down on the 27th, the pressure would have been irresistible. Attorney General Robert Kennedy reportedly said in a 1964 interview that after the downing of the U-2 on 27 October, Ambassador Anatoly Dobrynin was warned that "if one more plane was destroyed, we would hit all the SAMs immediately, and probably the missiles as well, and we would probably follow that with an invasion." Former Treasury Secretary C. Douglas Dillon recalls that when the U-2 was shot down, it added enormously to the pressure to act. By Saturday the 27th, there was a clear majority in the Ex-

Comm in favor of taking military action.

The Soviet ambassador to Cuba, Aleksandr Alekseev, recounts that there were daily communications between Castro and Khrushchev from 23 to 27 October. Castro, he recalls, encouraged the Soviets to remain firm in keeping the missiles in Cuba. But it is not clear whether the Cubans were informed fully about Soviet deliberations and intentions, or even whether the Soviets may have misinformed the Cubans intentionally or inadvertently. . . .

The nature of the communications between Castro and Khrushchev take on added significance because of the way Khrushchev may have interpreted them, and how that influenced his behavior. An indication of why this is important comes from the controversy surrounding the most publicized cable, sent on 26 October by Castro. In Khrushchev's most recently released memoirs, he recalls that "Castro suggested that to prevent our nuclear missiles from being destroyed, we should launch a pre-emptive strike against the U.S. My comrades in the leadership and I realized that our friend Fidel totally failed to understand our purpose."

This communication from the Cuban leader, Khrushchev indicates, was an important factor in his decision to withdraw the missiles. Yet Soviet participants at a 1991 meeting of former officials from Cuba, the United States, and the Soviet Union, held in Antigua, explained that Castro's cable did not reach Khrushchev until 1:10 A.M. on 28 October, after he had decided to withdraw the missiles. Moreover, as indicated earlier, Castro's call for a preemptive attack was qualified by his assessment that the likely U.S. action would be an air strike, and that only a U.S. invasion should be met with a Soviet first strike. Still, in a letter to Castro on 30 October, Khrushchev provided evidence that he may have missed the subtlety in the Cuban's cable, because he writes: "In your cable of October 27 you proposed that we be the first to launch a nuclear strike against the territory of an enemy. You, of course, realized where that would have led. Rather than a simple strike, it would have been the start of a thermonuclear world war. Dear Comrade Fidel Castro, I consider this proposal of yours incorrect, although I understand your motivation."

What Khrushchev may have based his judgment on was a 27 October cable from the Soviet ambassador to Cuba, previewing the Castro cable that was to arrive later. It may have been on the basis of the ambassador's report that Khrushchev believed Castro was highly agitated, fearing an imminent invasion (although that would contrast with the several reports about Castro's general calmness). Alternately, the ambassador may merely have reported his assessment that an invasion was imminent, and an excited Khrushchev interpreted this in an extreme manner. Whatever the case, Castro's cable or its preview by the ambassador may have contributed to the Soviet leader's calculation that a speedy termination of the crisis was essential to avoid a major conflagration. . . .

After the Brink

What Americans call the "Cuban missile crisis," and the Soviets call the "Caribbean crisis," the Cubans call the "October crisis." This nomenclature is used to signify that the period in October, when the United States and Soviet Union were on the brink of nuclear catastrophe, was only one of several crises that took on catastrophic proportions for the Cubans.

In reality, the crisis did not end on 28 October for either the United States or the Soviet Union. The Kennedy-Khrushchev agreements had to be implemented and Cuba became very much a part of that process. Until 20 November, the U.S. Strategic Air Command remained on alert at Defense Condition (DefCon) 2 (the state of full readiness for war); other forces were held at DefCon3, and the naval quarantine was maintained in place. Just as any of several incidents before 28 October might have led to an escalating exchange, so too the situation until 20 November remained very dangerous.

The United States asserted that the Kennedy-Khrushchev agreement required an on-site UN inspection in Cuba to assure that the offensive weapons were being dismantled and returned to the Soviet Union. Included in the list of weapons were all the IL-28 bombers. Cuba, in turn, insisted that it would not permit inspection on its soil, and that the IL-28s were Cuban property, given to Cuba by the Soviet Union. Castro asserted that the Soviet Union had no authority to negotiate with the United States about inspection procedures or about the return of the bombers. Instead, he announced, Cuba would be willing to negotiate on the basis of five demands: that the United States end the economic embargo, cease subversive activities against Cuba, end the "pirate" attacks from bases in the United States and Puerto Rico, cease violations of Cuban airspace, and return Guantanamo Naval Base. . . .

Castro's sense at the time was that the bargain was struck too readily, without adequate assurances, and that the United States would take advantage of loopholes to undermine Cuban security. This apparently was confirmed for him when the United States included the IL-28s in the demand for removal of offensive weapons, and later when Komar patrol boats were on the list Ambassador Adlai Stevenson presented to Anastas Mikoyan.

Similarly, on 8 November a Mongoose terrorist squad bombed a Cuban factory. Its action was supposedly unauthorized, because Mongoose activities had been suspended on 30 October. Apparently the group had been dispatched to Cuba before the official suspension of activities, and could not be recalled. The attack undoubtedly reinforced the Cuban belief that the United States could not be trusted. Their first inclination would have been to conclude that the U.S. destabilization campaign was still at work. It is also possible that they viewed the attach as a ploy in the U.S.-Soviet negotiations concerning the removal of the IL-28s and on-site inspection. However, since Cuba was not a party to the negotiations, Cuban officials would have been unlikely to interpret the Mongoose bombing merely as a negotiating tactic.

When the United States deals with small countries, the use of force or the threat of force to achieve political ends can have "exaggerated" consequences.

In part it was concern over Mongoose raids that led Cuba to be adamant about the violation of airspace, because U.S. surveillance planes had been used to support sabotage operations. In his 15 November letter to [U.N. Secretary General] U Thant, Castro observed that "photographs taken by the [U.S.] spying planes serve for guidance in sabotage." He also asserted that low-level flights went over "our military defences and photograph not only the dismantled strategic missile installations but in fact our entire territory." Clearly, Cuba saw the flights as continued preparation for an invasion and Castro warned that surveillance craft would be destroyed.

Notably, Cuba did make an offer—on 25 November, after the crisis ended—to allow UN inspection on its soil. But it was based on the pointed condition of a reciprocal inspection of alleged émigré training camps in the United States and Puerto Rico, to assure that they were being dismantled.

The agreement with Kennedy left no room for Cuban participation and offered Cuba no opportunity to bring the United States to the bargaining table over matters of vital Cuban interest. A simple demand that the United States talk to Cuba at the moment when the world stood at the brink would have been difficult for Kennedy to reject. Castro no doubt found it difficult to fathom why Khrushchev would not include such a demand in his deal. This contributed to Castro's anger as much as the fact that Khrushchev did not notify him before announcing that the missiles would be removed.

Had Castro been involved in negotiations, there is little doubt that a resolution of the crisis would have been more difficult. Some argue that his "adventurism" led to the very placement of the missiles of Cuba, and from this point of view he would have been an irascible negotiator. Personality aside, though, if Cuba had been included in negotiations, its interests would then need to have been taken into account. . . .

Rethinking the Crisis

For several years after the Cuban missile crisis there was a conventional wisdom, articulated by Arthur Schlesinger, Jr., that the crisis was resolved through a "combination of toughness and restraint, of will, nerve and wisdom, so brilliantly controlled, so matchlessly calibrated." Yet we have come to realize now that luck may have been just as important, because so much was uncontrolled and so many incidents may have precipitated a clash inadvertently. By adding a Cuban perspective to the picture of missile crisis decision making, it becomes even clearer that the potential for miscalculation was great. Cuban leaders were new to "high" politics, as one Cuban delegate to the Moscow conference said in a 1989 interview. They did not have experience in dealing with matters that had global implications. None of the leaders involved in the crisis wanted a nuclear war, but none was able to be the fully rational actors that some would believe they could have been. Because they lacked considerable information necessary for rational action, Cuban officials were probably the worst informed of any of the actors in the crisis.

The emerging view about how the missile crisis was managed has led to a new dictum. As [Defense Secretary] Robert McNamara said in 1987, "Crisis management is a very uncertain and very difficult thing to do, and therefore, you've got to avoid the crises in the first place." The first step in such an effort is improvement in communications between adversaries. This was appreciated at the time, and the so-called hotline was installed soon after the crisis. But what could the United States have communicated honestly to Cuba about Operation Mongoose and the attempted assassinations of Prime Minister Castro that would have assuaged Cuba's fears? Improved communications can reduce misunderstanding; but Cuba seems to have understood U.S. intentions quite well.

This suggests a lesson from the crisis that has been overlooked, because prior analyses have focused only on the two superpowers. For a small power, conventional warfare may be as threatening as nuclear warfare is to the United States. And a small power is likely to take whatever steps are necessary to reduce the threat. Thus, when the United States deals with small countries, the use of force or the threat of force to achieve political ends can have "exaggerated" consequences.

In reviewing recent scholarship about the missile crisis, political scientist David Bobrow aptly concluded that "narratives should include . . . all those actors with latitude to act," as well as "the context of the story as construed by each of those actors." The validity of his recommendation is clear from the analysis here: Only by reintroducing Cuba into the Cuban missile crisis can we hope to develop a picture of the full significance of the crisis itself.

Chapter 3

Lessons and Revelations

1

Kennedy Benefited from Listening to Diverse Opinions

Robert F. Kennedy

Robert F. Kennedy, President Kennedy's younger brother, served as Attorney General under Kennedy's administration. He was one of the members of the Executive Committee that advised the president on how the United States should respond to the Soviet challenge. In the essay, he stresses the importance of the variety of opinions that went into the discussion between the president and his advisers. He is convinced that in such a grave dispute, one party should put himself in the shoes of the other to understand his position better. Acting on behalf of the president, he held secret negotiations with Soviet Ambassador Anatoly Dobrynin at the height of the crisis. He was assassinated in 1968, five years after President Kennedy's death.

I often thought afterward of some of the things we learned from this confrontation. The time that was available to the President and his advisers to work secretly, quietly, privately, developing a course of action and recommendations for the President, was essential. If our deliberations had been publicized, if we had had to make a decision in twenty-four hours, I believe the course that we ultimately would have taken would have been quite different and filled with far greater risks. The fact that we were able to talk, debate, argue, disagree, and then debate some more was essential in choosing our ultimate course. Such time is not always pre-

Excerpted from *Thirteen Days: A Memoir of the Cuban Missile Crisis*, by Robert F. Kennedy (New York: W.W. Norton & Company, 1969). Copyright © 1968 by McCall Corporation. Reprinted with permission of W.W. Norton & Company, Inc.

sent, although, perhaps surprisingly, on most occasions of great crisis it is; but when it is, it should be utilized.

But more than time is necessary. I believe our deliberations proved conclusively how important it is that the President have the recommendations and opinions of more than one individual, of more than one department, and of more than one point of view. Opinion, even fact itself, can best be judged by conflict, by debate. There is an important element missing when there is unanimity of viewpoint. . . .

It is also important that different departments of government be represented. . . .

At the missile-crisis conferences [the President] made certain there were experts and representatives of different points of view.

During the Cuban missile crisis, the President not only received information from all the significant departments, but went to considerable lengths to ensure that he was not insulated from individuals or points of view because of rank or position. He wanted the advice of his Cabinet officers, but he also wanted the opinion of those who were connected with the situation itself. He wanted to hear from Secretary [Dean] Rusk, but he also wished to hear from Tommy Thompson, former (and now again) Ambassador to the Soviet Union, whose advice on the Russians and predictions as to what they would do were uncannily accurate and whose advice and recommendations were surpassed by none; from Ed Martin, Assistant Secretary for Latin America, who organized our effort to secure the backing of the Latin American countries; also from George Ball, the Under Secretary of State, whose advice and judgment were invaluable. He wanted to hear from Secretary [Robert] McNamara, but he wanted to hear also from Under Secretary [Roswell] Gilpatric, whose ability, knowledge, and judgment he sought in every serious crisis.

On other occasions, I had frequently observed efforts being made to exclude certain individuals from participating in a meeting with the President because they held a different point of view. Often, the President would become aware of this fact and enlarge the meetings to include other opinions. At the missile-crisis conferences he made certain there were experts and representatives of different points of view. President Kennedy wanted people who raised questions, who criticized, on whose judgment he could rely, who presented an intelligent point of view, regardless of their rank or viewpoint.

He wanted to hear presented and challenged all the possible consequences of a particular course of action. The first step might appear sensible, but what would be the reaction of our adversaries and would we actually stand to gain? . . .

It was to obtain an unfettered and objective analysis that he frequently, and in critical times, invited Secretary of the Treasury Douglas Dillon, for whose wisdom he had such respect; Kenny O'Donnell, his appointment secretary; Ted Sorensen; and, at times, former Secretary of State Dean Acheson, former Secretary of Defense Robert Lovett, former High Commissioner of Germany John McCloy, and others. They asked the difficult questions; they made others defend their position; they presented a different point of view; and they were skeptical.

I think this was more necessary in the military field than any other. President Kennedy was impressed with the effort and dedicated manner in which the military responded— the Navy deploying its vessels into the Caribbean; the Air Force going on continuous alert; the Army and the Marines moving their soldiers and equipment into the southeastern part of the U.S.; and all of them alert and ready for combat.

Restraining the Generals

But he was distressed that the representatives with whom he met, with the notable exception of General [Maxwell] Taylor, seemed to give so little consideration to the implications of steps they suggested. They seemed always to assume that if the Russians and the Cubans would not respond or, if they did, that a war was in our national interest. One of the Joint Chiefs of Staff once said to me he believed in a preventive attack against the Soviet Union. On that fateful Sunday morning when the Russians answered they were withdrawing their missiles, it was suggested by one high military adviser that we attack Monday in any case. Another felt that we had in some way been betrayed.

President Kennedy was disturbed by this inability to look beyond the limited military field. When we talked about this later, he said we had to remember that they were trained to fight and to wage war—that was their life. Perhaps we would feel even more concerned if they were always opposed to using arms or military means—for if they would not be willing, who would be? But this experience pointed out for us all the importance of civilian direction and control and the importance of raising probing questions to military recommendations.

It was for these reasons, and many more, that President Kennedy regarded Secretary McNamara as the most valuable public servant in his Administration and in the government.

From all this probing and examination—of the military, State Department, and their recommendations—President Kennedy hoped that he would at least be prepared for the foreseeable contingencies and know that—although no course of action is ever completely satisfactory—he had made his decision based on the best possible information. His conduct of the missile crisis showed how important this kind of skeptical probing and questioning could be.

The Importance of Allies

It also showed how important it was to be respected around the world, how vital it was to have allies and friends. Now, five years later, I discern a feeling of isolationism in Congress and through the country, a feeling that we are too involved with other nations, a resentment of the fact that we do not have greater support in Vietnam, an impression that our AID program is useless and our alliances dangerous. I think it would be well to think back to those days in October 1962. . . .

It was the vote of the Organization of American States [OAS] that gave a legal basis for the quarantine. Their willingness to follow the leadership of the United States was a heavy and unexpected blow to [Premier] Khrushchev. It had a major psychological and practical effect on the Russians and changed our position from that of an outlaw acting in violation of international law into a country acting in accordance with twenty allies legally protecting their position.

Similarly, the support of our NATO allies—the rapid public acceptance of our position by [West German Chancellor] Adenauer, [French President] de Gaulle, and [British Prime Minister] Macmillan—was of great importance. They accepted our recitation of the facts without question and publicly supported our position without reservation. Had our relationship of trust and mutual respect not been present, had our NATO [defense alliance in Europe] allies been skeptical about what we were doing and its implications for them, and had Khrushchev thus been able to split off the NATO countries or even one of our chief allies, our position would have been seriously undermined.

The final lesson of the Cuban missile crisis is the importance of placing ourselves in the other country's shoes.

Even in Africa, support from a number of countries that had been considered antagonistic toward the United States was of great significance. With a naval quarantine around Cuba, our military reported, Soviet planes could still fly atomic warheads into Cuba. To do so they had to refuel in West Africa, and the critical countries with sufficiently large airports and the necessary refueling facilities were Guinea and Senegal. President Kennedy sent our two Ambassadors to see the Presidents of those two countries. . . .

In short, our friends, our allies, and, as Thomas Jefferson said, a respect for the opinions of mankind, are all vitally important. We cannot be an island even if we wished; nor can we successfully separate ourselves from the rest of the world. . . .

Putting Ourselves in the Other's Shoes

The final lesson of the Cuban missile crisis is the importance of placing ourselves in the other country's shoes. During the crisis, President Kennedy spent more time trying to determine the effect of a particular course of action on Khrushchev or the Russians than on any other phase of what he was doing. What guided all his deliberations was an effort not to disgrace Khrushchev, not to humiliate the Soviet Union, not to have them feel they would have to escalate their response because their national security or national interests so committed them.

This was why he was so reluctant to stop and search a Russian ship; this was why he was so opposed to attacking the missile sites. The Russians, he felt, would have to react militarily to such actions on our part.

Thus the initial decision to impose a quarantine rather than to attack; our decision to permit the *Bucharest* to pass; our decision to board a non-Russian vessel first; all these and many more were taken with a view to putting pressure on the Soviet Union but not causing a public humiliation.

Miscalculation and misunderstanding and escalation on one side bring a counterresponse. No action is taken against a powerful adversary in a vacuum. A government or people will fail to understand this only at their great peril. For that is how wars begin—wars that no one wants, no one intends, and no one wins.

Each decision that President Kennedy made kept this in mind. Always he asked himself: Can we be sure that Khrushchev understands what we feel to be our vital national interest? Has the Soviet Union had sufficient time to react soberly to a particular step we have taken? All action was judged against that standard—stopping a particular ship, sending low-flying planes, making a public statement.

Mutual Avoidance of War

President Kennedy understood that the Soviet Union did not want war, and they understood that we wished to avoid armed conflict. Thus, if hostilities were to come, it would be either because our national interests collided—which, because of their limited interests and our purposely limited objectives, seemed unlikely—or because of our failure or their failure to understand the other's objectives.

President Kennedy dedicated himself to making it clear to Khrushchev by word and deed—for both are important—that the U.S. had limited objectives and that we had no interest in accomplishing those objectives by adversely affecting the national security of the Soviet Union or by humiliating her.

Later, he was to say in his speech at American University in June of 1963: "Above all, while defending our own vital interests, nuclear powers must avert those confrontations which bring an adversary to the choice of either a humiliating defeat or a nuclear war."

During our crisis talks, he kept stressing the fact that we would indeed have war if we placed the Soviet Union in a position she believed would adversely affect her national security or such public humiliation that she lost the respect of her own people and countries around the globe. The missiles in Cuba, we felt, vitally concerned our national security, but not that of the Soviet Union.

This fact was ultimately recognized by Khrushchev, and this recognition, I believe, brought about his change in what, up to that time, had been a very adamant position. The President believed from the start that the Soviet Chairman was a rational, intelligent man who, if given sufficient time and shown our determination, would alter his position. But there was always the chance of error, of mistake, miscalculation, or misunderstanding, and President Kennedy was committed to doing everything possible to lessen that chance on our side.

The possibility of the destruction of mankind was always in his mind. Someone once said that World War Three would be fought with atomic weapons and the next war with sticks and stones.

As mentioned before, Barbara Tuchman's *The Guns of August* had made a great impression on the President. "I am not going to follow a course which will allow anyone to write a comparable book about this time, *The Missiles of October*," he said to me that Saturday night, October 26. "If anybody is around to write after this, they are going to understand that we made every effort to find peace and every effort to give our adversary room to move. I am not going to push the Russians an inch beyond what is necessary."

After it was finished, he made no statement attempting to take credit for himself or for the Administration for what had occurred. He instructed all members of the Ex Comm and government that no interview should be given, no statement made, which would claim any kind of victory. He respected Khrushchev for properly determining what was in his own country's interest and what was in the interest of mankind. If it was a triumph, it was a triumph for the next generation and not for any particular government or people.

2

The Lessons of the Crisis Are Ambiguous

Robert Smith Thompson

Robert Smith Thompson argues that contrary to popular belief that the conclusion of the crisis brought resounding success for U.S. foreign policy, the country offered concessions, as well. He points to the country's giving up of the Jupiter missiles in Turkey, the eventual renunciation by the United States of any plans to invade Cuba, and the fact that Cuba today continues to exist. Thompson is the author of *Pledge to Destiny: Charles De Gaulle and the Rise of the Free French* and *A Time for War: Franklin D. Roosevelt and the Path to Pearl Harbor.*

"It can be said" of [President John F.] Kennedy, eulogized one editorialist, shortly after [his] funeral [in 1963],

> that he did not fear the weather, and did not trim his sail, but instead challenged the wind itself, to improve its direction and cause it to blow more softly and more kindly over the world and its people.

To that editorialist, as to much of "the world and its people," Kennedy's greatest challenge to the wind had come during the Cuban missile crisis; indeed the crisis had assumed mythic proportion. According to that legend, the Soviet Union, ever intent on burying America, had engineered Castro's revolution, turning Cuba into a Communist satellite, then treacherously and without just cause introducing missiles with which they intended to bring the U.S. to its knees. The legend continued: although caught by surprise by photos of the missiles, President Kennedy kept his cool. Assembling a team of advisers, he quickly devised the best strategy for getting the missiles out of Cuba. Succumbing neither to appeasement nor belligerence, he (1) kept all planning before his October 22 speech a secret, thereby avoiding any chance that the Soviets would be tipped off; then (2) he presented the Kremlin with a quarantine, an implied threat of force, and the face-saving device of a U.S. noninvasion pledge; and (3) he thereby induced [Chairman] Khrushchev to back down.

Having thus realized his overriding goal, the return of the global strategic balance to the status quo ante, Kennedy turned his attention to the cause of world peace. Abroad he became a good neighbor; at home he became a statesman.

Thus the myth. The reality was different.

Had Kennedy, becoming a statesman, ceased to be a politician? . . .

For domestic political reasons, Kennedy simply had *to stand up to Khrushchev.*

Had Kennedy, as he developed his missile crisis strategy, then risen above concern with his own political interest in being reelected President? No. When meeting with Excomm, of course, he was shrewd enough to stay off the subject of politics—the last thing he needed was to have John McCone or Lyndon Johnson leaking word that JFK had cooked up the whole thing for his own advantage. But McNamara understood. "I'll be quite frank," he said on October 16, 1962. "I don't think there is a military problem here. . . . This is a domestic political problem." For domestic political reasons, Kennedy simply *had* to stand up to Khrushchev.

Standing Up to Khrushchev

Had he indeed stood up to Khrushchev? Only in part. Kennedy was able to realize a compromise, trading the noninvasion pledge for the Cuban missile withdrawal, but *then* having to throw in the Turkish missile withdrawal. No wonder Robert Kennedy was so anxious to suppress written evidence of the Jupiter deal!

Had Kennedy, before October 15, 1962, had no idea of the presence of the missiles in Cuba? He would have had to be blind, deaf, and dumb not to know. [Central Intelligence Agency Director John] McCone had shown him the intelligence reports.

Had the Soviets deceived JFK about the presence of the missiles? Yes and no. They had promised not to introduce "offensive" missiles but had left open the option of deploying "defensive" ones; so the Kremlin did shade the truth. But Khrushchev had made clear, emphatically clear, that he intended to defend Cuba with missiles.

Had the Soviet deployment of missiles to Cuba been without just cause? And had Khrushchev intended, with those missiles, to bring the U.S. to its knees? If protecting an ally against invasion was a just cause, then Khrushchev had justice on his side. If Khrushchev wanted to bring the U.S. to its knees, he could have done so just as well from missiles in the Soviet bloc countries as from Cuba.

Had Kennedy truly been on the verge of invading Cuba? Nowhere do we find a document bearing his signature and saying, "Invade." What we do find in the archives, however, are plans for an invasion, massive proof of the buildup of an invasion, statements by top-ranking officials that they wanted to provoke [Cuban leader] Castro into providing a pretext (as with a strike at Guantánamo), and the fact that Operation Mongoose was to give Castro no choice but to provide that pretext. Late in the summer and early in the fall, 1962, we know, the Kennedy brothers were practically violent in their insistence that the Mongoose chieftains get moving.

Victory Was the Goal

So why the wish to invade Cuba? We might proceed, to use a term much employed in the Kennedy White House, along three "tracks."

First, the Kennedy track. As character molded the JFK presidential campaign, with Joseph Kennedy in the background, intent on victory at all costs and striving to master all relevant factors, so did the campaign mold the Kennedy presidency, with its effort above all else to portray JFK as a leader who could stand up to the Russians. The Kennedy White House, in today's parlance, tried to control the spin, the story line. But reality intruded. The Bay of Pigs was a failure. Laos was a failure. Vienna was a failure. JFK needed a victory, desperately. He had to regain control: he had to oust Castro.

Second, the worldwide track. From Hiroshima and Nagasaki onward, two American administrations, those of Presidents Truman and Eisenhower, had sought to perpetuate America's de facto postwar global empire: herein lay the meaning of the Truman Doctrine, NSC-68, the containment policy, and John Foster Dulles's threat of massive retaliation. Kennedy inherited this legacy of worldwide (or nearly worldwide) dominance—and he had no intention of letting that dominance go to pieces on his watch. So, like his predecessors, he believed that U.S. forces were required, and could prevail, wherever U.S. interests seemed to be threatened, or might be advanced. And down here was Castro, eluding that grasp.

Third, the Cuban track. In the imagination of Americans, Cuba throughout the century had been little more than an extension of Florida: the U.S.—so we believed— had liberated Cuba from Spain, had preserved the right (granted by God, or by the Platt Amendment, which amounted to the same thing) to intervene in Cuba (for Cuba's own good, of course), had brought to Cuba the benefits of baseball, tourism, and dollars. And all Cuba had had to do in return was to accept America's de facto control. But Fidel Castro had refused to accept such control. He thus was an outlaw. And, as in the old cowboy movies, you do not negotiate with outlaws. You shoot them down in front of the town saloon. Until the next week's episode, you have brought the bad guys under control.

In the imagination of Americans, . . . the U.S. . . . had liberated Cuba from Spain. . . . And all Cuba had to do in return was to accept Ameria's de facto control.

Each of these "tracks" helps explain why Kennedy's Cuban policy (which grew out of Eisenhower's Cuban policy, which grew out of Eisenhower's Guatemalan policy) evolved into a full-blown effort to invade the island. But the Cuban-American relationship, in the real world, was hardly a B-grade Hollywood cowboy flick. Or, if it was, then Nikita Khrushchev waddled into the theater, pushed his way up to the projection booth, and with a toss of one of his beefy hands, hurled the projector to the floor. The movie—the illusion of control—was over.

For Khrushchev had got away with doing the unthinkable: he had deterred American aggression. How? In the background of the Cuban missile crisis, always, was the one element of international affairs consistently beyond American control: Berlin. Had Khrushchev made a grab at Berlin, the U.S. could have done little to stop him; or the cost at least would have been sky-high. And, recognizing Khrushchev's advantage at Berlin, Kennedy, to get the Soviet missiles out of Cuba, caved in over the U.S. missiles in Turkey.

When confronted by aggression, . . . show flexibility over minor points, but never yield to major ones; . . . keep the bludgeon conveniently nearby.

Kennedy's court historians have pretended otherwise, denying that the Jupiters were part of the deal. But they have lost control of the evidence. And the evidence exists in Washington. The National Security Archive, housed in a building next door to the Brookings Institution, just off Dupont Circle on Massachusetts Avenue, has collected all the documents, so far declassified, on the Cuban missile crisis. The documents are available for all to see. What they show is this: Khrushchev beat Kennedy in Vienna. And he beat him again in Cuba.

Model for Vietnam and Iraq

In the end, therefore, we confront the "lessons" of the Cuban missile crisis. These "lessons" fall into two groups, those "learned" by the Kennedy administration and those "learned" by America ever since.

As the officials of the Kennedy administration rested, then returned to their duties, they shifted their attention from Cuba to Vietnam. To Southeast Asia they applied four principles they had gleaned from the Caribbean: (1) that success in an international crisis was "largely a matter of national guts"; (2) that the "opponent would yield to superior force"; (3) that presidential control of force can be "suitable, selective, swift, effective, and responsive" to the situation's demands; and (4) that "crisis management and execution are too dangerous and events move too rapidly for anything but the tightest secrecy." Framed, as it were, as plaques on the walls of the Oval Office, these "lessons" underlay President Johnson's bombing of Hanoi in 1965 and President Nixon's bombing of Cambodia in 1973.

Nearly two decades later, in the winter of 1990–1991, the United States entered the Persian Gulf War. Justifying that belligerency, Les Alpin, Democratic Representative from Wisconsin and chairman of the House Committee on Armed Services, wrote in *The Washington Post:*

> The model [for President Bush to follow] is the Cuban missile crisis of 1962. In that crisis, as in this one, the United States sought to restore the status quo ante— no Soviet missiles capable of reaching the United States in Cuba.

> Then, as now, there was no backing down on the basic demand. The missiles had to go then, and Iraq has to leave Kuwait now.

For three decades then the "lesson" of the Cuban missile crisis has persisted in the textbooks of our minds: when confronted by aggression, you hang tough, stay cool, show flexibility over minor points, but never yield on major ones; plan to operate with surgical precision, but keep the bludgeon conveniently nearby.

Yet are the "lessons" valid? The Cuban missile crisis hardly culminated in a grand victory; as a triumph for Kennedy it was, at best, ambiguous. And at worst? The Cuban missile crisis was the direct result, as the Soviets have reminded us repeatedly, of the American desire to overrun Cuba—to restore the status quo ante, the status quo of the "glory days" of Fulgencio Batista or even of Teddy Roosevelt.

The more appropriate lesson of the missile crisis might be in the ancient idea of hubris, pride, arrogance, and that these qualities lead to a fall. As sure that they could control the Caribbean and indeed the world as they had controlled their own campaign, the Kennedys found themselves, in the end, faced down by that stubby little peasant, Nikita Khrushchev.

President Kennedy had often turned for guidance to a book by Professor Richard Nedstadt, entitled *Presidential*

Power. But he also might have pondered a book by Eric Ambler, the English novelist. The book was called *A Coffin for Demetrios.* In it Ambler wrote:

> The situation in which a person, imagining fondly that he is in charge of his own destiny, is, in fact, the sport of circumstances beyond his control, is always fascinating. It is the essential element in most good theater. . . .

But the ultimate lesson of the Cuban missile crisis is what you see, nowadays, when you fly into the Havana airport. As your airplane lowers over the Caribbean, you look out the cabin window. You see the sky, you see the sea, you feel the aircraft touch down; and then, as it seems to rush by the window, you see it. It is mounted on a pile of what looks like cement blocks. Its substructure is a jumble of girders and cables, and from its bottom extend what resembles four fins. It is cylindrical and long, about sixty feet high. It stands aloft, at a slight angle, and the conical tip seems to be pointed toward the United States of America.

As your airplane reaches the Havana terminal, you realize what you have just seen—a Soviet missile, one of Khrushchev's rockets that did *not* come out. It seems to have no military significance. It does symbolize, though, the real meaning of the Cuban missile crisis. True to his upbringing and indeed to the creed of the American nation, President Kennedy had been sure he could do anything—he could conquer the White House, he could vanquish Castro, he could control the risks. Yet in the end it was Castro who survived.

3

Understanding Kennedy and Khrushchev

James G. Blight and David A. Welch

This essay offers insights into the decisions made by Kennedy and Khrushchev in resolving the crisis. At the outset, each leader was outraged by the other's actions, but as they moved on and saw the similarity of their positions and the gravity of their responsibility, they realized that their predicament was mutual. The following essay draws on new information provided by Soviet officials who were involved in the crisis. James G. Blight was assistant director at Harvard University's Center for Science and International Affairs at the time of writing. He is the author of *Cuba on the Brink: Castro, the Missile Crisis and the Soviet Collapse* and *Politics of Illusion: The Bay of Pigs Invasion Reconsidered*, as well as other works on psychology and psychoanalysis. David A. Welch is the author of works on internationalism and on the Cuban missile crisis. He was a research fellow at Harvard's Center for Science and International Affairs at the time of writing.

If President Kennedy and Chairman Khrushchev performed poorly at crisis avoidance, it must be said that they fared much better at crisis management. That they did so despite their evident inability to communicate and to understand each other prior to the crisis is nothing less than astounding.

We have every reason to believe that Khrushchev was as shocked at Kennedy's October 22 address as Kennedy was at the discovery of Soviet missiles in Cuba. For several hours, there was no response from Moscow; Soviet diplomacy was thrown into complete disarray. Anatoly Dobrynin in Washington and Valerian Zorin at the UN were caught completely unprepared to respond, because they themselves had not been aware of the deployment. Khrushchev, believing either that the secrecy surrounding the deployment would hold or that the United States would use quiet diplomacy to voice its objections if the missiles were discovered prematurely, seems indeed to have been caught, as Dean Rusk put it in his interview, with his scenario down.

When Khrushchev finally responded, he was clearly outraged. The first salvo of his October 23 barrage was the charge that "the United States has openly taken the path of grossly violating the United Nations Charter, the path of violating international norms of freedom of navigation on the high seas, the path of aggressive actions both against Cuba and against the Soviet Union." Wednesday's *Pravda* [official newspaper of the Communist Party] headlines screamed: "The unleashed American aggressors must be stopped!" and "Hands off Cuba!" Of course, the ExComm expected a clamor of this kind; what they did not know was that Khrushchev's reaction to Kennedy's speech of October 22 was every bit as violent, irrational, and dangerous as the doves had feared it might be.

According to dissident Soviet historian Roy Medvedev, Khrushchev immediately issued an order to speed up work on the missile sites so as to make them operational as soon as possible. Though Kennedy intended the quarantine to persuade Khrushchev to halt construction of the missile sites and defuse the crisis through negotiation, Khrushchev's fury inclined him to do just the opposite. But even more ominously, according to Medvedev's account, Khrushchev began "denouncing the naval blockade as banditry, the folly of degenerate imperialism . . . [and] issued orders to the captains of Soviet ships as they were approaching the blockade zone to ignore it and to hold course for the Cuban ports." If this order had held, war between the superpowers would probably have commenced at sea, shortly after ten o'clock on Wednesday morning, October 24, 1962, several hundred miles off the coast of Cuba.

According to Medvedev, it was Anastas Mikoyan who, as Soviet ships approached the quarantine line, preempted Khrushchev's order to run the blockade, and ordered Soviet ships to stop just short of the quarantine line—prompting Dean Rusk to utter his famous line: "We were eyeball to eyeball and the other fella just blinked." Medvedev's account has attracted surprisingly little attention in the West, perhaps in part because it appears in an unlikely place for scholars of the missile crisis to look: in a book on Stalin's associates. And, until recently, there has been no independent confirmation of Medvedev's account, so we have been unable to gauge its accuracy. But, shortly after the [1987] Cambridge conference, Sergo Mikoyan confirmed to us that Medvedev's account is factual. Khrushchev's blink may have come just in the nick of time.

Similar Reaction

Khrushchev's reaction to the announcement of the quarantine was similar in many respects to President Kennedy's (and most of his advisors') initial reaction to the discovery of Soviet missiles in Cuba. On both sides, outrage and anger were clearly the dominant emotions. Not surprisingly, then, the initial inclination on both sides was to respond belligerently. There can be no mistaking the hawkish tone of the discussions in the White House on October 16: the President, for example, seemed at one point to have decided at a minimum to order a surgical air strike against the Soviet missiles; his brother Robert—who in *Thirteen Days* portrayed himself as a leader of the doves—proposed to engineer an incident to use as a pretext for an attack, suggesting that it might be a good idea to "sink the *Maine* again or something." But by October 22 the President and his advisors had had time to consider their options, reevaluate the chain of events that had led to the crisis, ponder Soviet motives and intentions, and absorb the awesome implications of irreversible actions and mistakes. In those six days, they seem to have become aware of the monumental misjudgments both they and the Soviets had made, and they came to appreciate some of the dangers associated with that fact. It is therefore with a slight tone of injured innocence that the President, in his message to Khrushchev on October 22, took pains to point out that "it was in order to avoid any incorrect assessment on the part of your Government with respect to Cuba that I publicly stated that if certain developments in Cuba took place, the United States would do whatever must be done to protect its own security and that of its allies," and that "this minimum response should not be taken as a basis . . . for any misjudgment on your part"—as though the accuracy and prudence of Khrushchev's judgments could be improved by urging him not to misjudge.

Khrushchev's opening salvo clearly disheartened Kennedy; in his fury, Khrushchev was not getting the point. He was not seeing that misjudgments had gotten them both into the predicament in the first place, and he certainly had not yet appreciated the potential for the confrontation to take on an uncontrollable momentum of its own. Kennedy should not have been surprised; he had had more than a week to learn his lessons, and Khrushchev had had but a few hours. But the President could not afford to wait very long; he had to try to speed Khrushchev's learning process. In reply to Khrushchev's October 23 statement, therefore, Kennedy poignantly urged "that we both show prudence and do nothing to allow events to make the situation more difficult to control than it already is." By urging that they *both* show prudence, Kennedy sought to communicate the mutuality of their predicament, and the cooperative dimension of the requirements for its resolution.

They recognized at last that they . . . faced common dangers; and that, more than anything else, they shared a common interest in resolving the confrontation on mutually satisfactory terms.

Khrushchev very nearly did not get the point in time. But by October 26 Khrushchev and Kennedy had "clicked," as Khrushchev's letter of that date clearly indicates. The two leaders had finally come to see their predicament in approximately the same light: they recognized at last that they were symmetrically placed; that they faced common dangers; and that, more than anything else, they shared a common interest in resolving the confrontation on mutually satisfactory terms. They did so by virtue of being, as Khrushchev put it, "invested with authority, trust and responsibility" to secure the peace.

I have received your letter of October 25. From your letter I got the feeling that you have some understanding of the situation which has developed and a sense of responsibility. I appreciate this. . . . I can see, Mr. President, that you also are not without a sense of anxiety for the fate of the world. . . . Should war indeed break out, it would not be in our power to contain or stop it, for such is the logic of war. I have taken part in two wars, and I know that war ends only when it has rolled through cities and villages, sowing death and destruction everywhere. . . . You and I should not now pull on the ends of the rope in which you have tied a knot of war, because the harder you and I pull, the tighter this knot will become. And a time may come when this knot is tied so tight that the person who tied it is no longer capable of untying it, and then the knot will have to be cut.

Khrushchev's more conciliatory and cooperative tone was echoed in the headlines of *Pravda*, which underwent a remarkable transformation between October 25 ("The aggressive designs of the United States imperialists must be foiled. Peace on earth must be defended and strengthened!") and October 26 ("Everything to prevent war," with an editorial entitled "Reason must prevail").

In his letter of October 26, Khrushchev vaguely offered to settle on terms that Kennedy and the ExComm could accept: the missiles in Cuba would be withdrawn in return for an American pledge not to invade the island. Khrushchev, it seems, had made up his mind that securing one of his goals—the defense of Cuba—was all that he could reasonably hope for under the present circumstances, and that redressing the strategic imbalance was obviously going to have to wait. But then something unexpected happened, according to [Georgi] Shaknazarov at the Cambridge meeting; Dobrynin informed Moscow that the United States might be willing to trade Jupiter missiles in Turkey for SS-4s and SS-5s in Cuba.

The circumstances surrounding the missile-trade proposal remain unclear. "Anatoly Dobrynin," said Shaknazarov, "told me that the Turkish idea was born here, in the Soviet Embassy, in a conversation, maybe with Robert Kennedy. It was suggested to Moscow, and then it came back." The only conversation Robert Kennedy had had with Dobrynin prior to the evening of October 27, which was after the proposal was made, occurred on October 23; and there is no evidence that a missile trade was discussed at that time. According to Arthur Schlesinger's account of the meeting, however, Robert Kennedy did make a remark that Dobrynin could possibly have interpreted later to mean that some such trade was possible. "The Attorney General noted," Schlesinger writes, "that the American President had met Khrushchev's request for the withdrawal of American troops from Thailand." This remark, obviously intended by Robert Kennedy to remind Dobrynin of the President's reasonableness and willingness to compromise, may have provided Dobrynin with what he took to be a clue to mutually acceptable terms of settlement. Dobrynin may also have been paying attention to other sources, however. It is possible, for example, that he mistakenly concluded that journalist Walter Lippmann was speaking for the American government when he proposed a Cuban-Turkish missile swap on October 25. Confirmation that the Soviet Embassy had picked up on Lippmann's proposal came when John Scali was sent to ask Aleksandr Fomin why the (acceptable) proposal of October 26 had been superceded by the missile-trade proposal before the President had even had a chance to reply; Fomin is reported to have mentioned that Lippmann himself had proposed it. It is clear, however, that the full story of the missile-trade proposal has yet to be told. Shaknazarov was evidently uncertain at the Cambridge meeting about Dobrynin's source, and the issue will probably remain unresolved until Dobrynin speaks to the issue himself.

They never appreciated the symmetry of their position until they were forced to "stare down the gun barrel of nuclear war" together.

The genesis of the missile-trade idea may be puzzling, but Khrushchev's decision to propose it—publicly, no less—is downright mystifying. At the Cambridge conference, Mikoyan suggested that the Foreign Ministry—and by implication Andrei Gromyko—may have convinced Khrushchev that an American non-invasion pledge was an insufficient quid pro quo, or that it would be both possible and desirable to demand more. It is conceivable, perhaps, that Khrushchev merely intended to use it as a lever for securing Kennedy's agreement on his previous offer by trying to make it look more attractive against the background of toughening terms. Whatever his thinking, the missile-swap proposal of October 27 was, as Tatu notes, "the most important Soviet blunder during the entire crisis." It threw a wrench into the delicate negotiations by forcing Kennedy and the ExComm to waste time and energy trying to ascertain which of Khrushchev's proposals was operative, and debating the merits and implications of the new one, even as events began to look as if they were spinning out of control. The missile-trade proposal also enraged both Cuba and Turkey, who had no intention of being treated as bargaining chips. It may be that Khrushchev simply had not thought through the implications of the proposal; "irrational reasons" may have been at work here as well as in his decision to deploy missiles to Cuba in the first place. But, whatever the explanation, he committed a serious gaffe at the climax of the confrontation.

A Dangerous Phase

As the ExComm agonized over Khrushchev's new initiative on October 27, word reached Washington that a U-2 reconnaissance plane had been shot down by a surface-to-air missile [SAM] fired from Cuba. The crisis seemed to have moved into a new, more dangerous phase. The circumstances surrounding the shoot-down of the U-2 have always been unclear. Many members of the ExComm appear to have believed that it signaled a deliberate escalation of the crisis. Jorge Dominguez suggests, based on his reading of Cuban sources, that Cubans had gained control of the SAMs as a matter of course some months earlier, and thus that Cubans were responsible, though Soviets probably executed the order to shoot, because only they at that point had the technical competence to operate the batteries. Former Castro associate and former editor of *Revolución*, Carlos Franqui, reported in his memoir that Castro had told him he had personally pushed the button that downed the U-2. Castro himself has recently returned to espousing a view he has held from time to time, that the Soviets controlled the SAMs and that he has no idea whether Moscow ordered it or not.

Fortuitously, on the day the Cambridge meeting convened for its opening dinner, a long and detailed article on the U-2 shoot-down appeared in *The Washington Post.* Drawn partly from an interview conducted with former Defense Department analyst Daniel Ellsberg, who was himself citing classified material from a post-crisis study of the event he had carried out for Robert McNamara, the article claimed that on October 26, 1962, a unit from the Cuban army attacked and overran the Soviet-controlled SAM site at Los Angeles, in Cuba, killing many Soviets and seizing control of the site. According to Ellsberg, the Cubans held the site until Soviets retook it the next day, but not before Cubans had fired the SAM that brought down the American U-2. Thus, Ellsberg implied, on the most dangerous day of the nuclear age, "a Cuban finger was on the button." Cubans had nearly provoked a superpower war.

Sergo Mikoyan unequivocally denies that Cuban and Soviet troops fought for control of the Los Angeles SAM site, though he has suggested in conversation that the cable on which Ellsberg rests his case may indicate that a Cuban exile group—or perhaps even a roving "Mongoose" team— may have been active in the area at that time. But it is inconceivable to him that a conflict between Cubans and Soviets could have escaped his notice, since he was with his father in Cuba at the conclusion of the crisis. At the Cambridge conference, Mikoyan seemed to have other reasons for rejecting Ellsberg's thesis, too, though he was evidently reticent to discuss them.

Spinning Out of Control

Shortly after the Cambridge meeting, CBS News made public the fact that a prominent Cuban defector, General Rafael del Piño, had told the CIA in his debriefing that a Soviet officer shot down Major Anderson's U-2. General del Piño was close to Castro throughout the missile crisis and is probably better informed about Cuban military affairs during that period than anyone else. His account, therefore, is prima facie credible. In attempting to confirm del Piño's claim, we discussed the question again privately with Sergo Mikoyan, whose reticence quickly vanished. He identified the Soviet officer responsible for the U-2 shoot-down as General Igor D. Statsenko, then a senior Soviet officer in Cuba. According to his own account, his reluctance to discuss the matter in detail at the Cambridge conference stemmed from a promise he had made to Statsenko not to divulge his identity while he was alive. Ironically, Statsenko died shortly after the conference itself.

The circumstances under which Statsenko made his ill-fated decision remain unclear. He apparently told Mikoyan that he had "two minutes" in which to decide whether or not to shoot—clearly not enough time to consult Moscow. But if there had been standing orders for him not to shoot, why would the predicament arise in the first place? We can only imagine that Statsenko believed some sort of American attack was already under way. It is not inconceivable that rumors to that effect circulated and unnerved Soviet forces in Cuba, who were, after all, thousands of miles from home, exposed on an island just ninety miles away from the United States, encircled by the U.S. Navy, and ordered to sit with their hands tied as Castro, shooting at everything in sight with his antiaircraft batteries, did his unwitting best to provoke an attack. The psychological climate was therefore ripe for panic; and the United States was doing its best to flex its muscles in the region as visibly as possible.

If there is such a thing as "nuclear learning,"
. . . Kennedy and Khrushchev provide the
textbook case.

Whatever the cause of Statsenko's panic, it is fortunate that both the ExComm and Nikita Khrushchev had by that time already tuned in to the dangers of accidents, inadvertencies, and breakdowns in command and control. The ExComm was therefore able to take the shoot-down surprisingly in stride, and Khrushchev, we may surmise, was able to appreciate that he could not afford to prolong the crisis indefinitely without risking—or inviting—a clash between Soviet and American forces, or another unauthorized attack on an American plane. Robert Kennedy was very clear in telling Dobrynin on October 27 that the United States could not accept the loss of another aircraft without retaliation; Khrushchev was not inclined to test him.

Khrushchev must have realized that his position was no

longer tenable and that further delays were unwarranted. It was time to settle. As Burlatsky said at the Cambridge meeting, he had no "effective alternative" for responding to an American attack on Cuba. While it may or may not have been a *casus belli* between the superpowers—the Soviets at the Cambridge conference debated this point, and no doubt there would have been some debate also in Moscow—Khrushchev and his colleagues could not risk having to resolve the ambiguity one way or another. It is hardly surprising, then, that near-panic seized the small group working with Khrushchev at his dacha outside Moscow, as they feverishly composed a brief reply to President Kennedy's October 27 letter and to Robert Kennedy's "ultimatum," rushed it to Radio Moscow, and took a specially secured elevator to the sixth floor in order to meet what they took to be the President's deadline for a decision. It was time to cash in the chips and go home.

The Educations of Kennedy and Khrushchev

Why were Kennedy and Khrushchev so poor at crisis avoidance, yet so capable of effective crisis management, even when events conspired to defeat them? The answer, it seems, is that they never appreciated the symmetry of their position until they were forced to "stare down the gun barrel of nuclear war" together. Khrushchev's letter of October 26 had hit the nail squarely on the head: he and Kennedy shared an awesome responsibility in the Cuban missile crisis, a responsibility no two men had ever had to share before. The weight of their misunderstandings and their different cultures, ideologies, faiths, backgrounds, and national interests—which had proven to be such impediments to meaningful and successful communication before the crisis—was nothing compared to the weight of the responsibility they shared during the crisis. Their joint responsibility for the survival of their nations and the peace of the world, and the powerful anxiety that accompanied it, overcame their ignorance, their prejudice, their bluster, and their blindness, when it really mattered.

It is instructive to recognize that they each experienced the crisis in much the same way, though on different timetables. Their initial reactions to their respective shocks—the discovery of Soviet missiles in Cuba for Kennedy, and the announcement of the quarantine for Khrushchev—were the same: outrage and anger. Both of them were initially inclined to react belligerently. After a period of reflection, however, in which righteous indignation gave way to introspection, and during which tempers cooled, they both came to see the predicament in approximately the same light. They both came to recognize that their chief enemy was the unpredictability and uncontrollability of events; that they could not afford to drive the other into a corner; and that their crucial task was to find a safe exit through which they could escape on short notice. With their minds thus focused on the mutuality of their predicament and on the cooperative requirements of its successful resolution, Kennedy and Khrushchev were able to develop an empathy that swept aside their earlier animosity, leaving behind a deep and abiding mutual respect. Of Kennedy, Khrushchev wrote, "his death was a great loss. He was gifted with the ability to resolve international conflicts by negotiation, as the whole world learned during the so-called Cuban crisis. Regardless of his youth, he was a real statesman. . . . He showed great flexibility and, together, we avoided disaster." Kennedy would doubtless have said the same of Khrushchev. Perhaps partly for this reason, neither of them was willing to declare victory at the conclusion of the crisis, even though Khrushchev, in his public statements, rarely shied away from making outrageous claims about other matters, and even though most of the rest of the world thought Kennedy clearly had something to crow about.

Time Was Essential

If there is such a thing as "nuclear learning," then surely Kennedy and Khrushchev provide the textbook case. But it is important to recognize that, even though they learned their lessons quickly, they very nearly did not learn them quickly enough. Robert Kennedy writes:

> The time that was available to the President and his advisers to work secretly, quietly, privately, developing a course of action and recommendations for the President, was essential. If our deliberations had been publicized, if we had had to make a decision in twenty-four hours, I believe the course that we ultimately would have taken would have been quite different and filled with far greater risks. The fact that we were able to

talk, debate, argue, disagree, and then debate some more was essential in choosing our ultimate course.

One might be tempted to think that Robert Kennedy is suggesting here that time was essential because it was necessary for the full exploration of the available options and their implications; but, . . . this was not the way in which the Ex-Comm used its time. The time was needed for the President and his advisors to learn. They needed time for their tempers to cool; they needed time to realize the weight of their responsibility; they needed time to recognize the dangers of the misperceptions and misjudgments that had brought them to the crisis in the first place, and the multidimensionality of the danger which they now faced. Had they not had that time, the President might indeed have found a *Maine* to sink, and the crisis, as Dean Rusk remarked, would have been "infinitely more dangerous."

The delay between the President's October 22 speech and the time when the quarantine went into effect—thirty-nine hours—may have been unavoidable for diplomatic reasons (the OAS [Organization of American States] still had to vote on the quarantine resolution), but there can be no question that it was vital. If Khrushchev had not had thirty-nine hours in which to settle down, his order to run the blockade might not have been rescinded. Similarly, if the U-2 shoot-down had occurred on October 17, rather than on October 27, the President's mind might not yet have been focused on the dangers it posed, and in his outrage he might not have been able to take it in stride. If the events of the Cuban missile crisis, therefore, had taken place over a three-day period, rather than a thirteen-day period, war between the superpowers might have been all but unavoidable, because Kennedy and Khrushchev would not have had time to learn their lessons.

That Kennedy and Khrushchev had so many lessons to learn—about each other, about the origins of crises, about the risks of war, and about crisis resolution—was a function of the fact that they started from such a low base level. U.S.-Soviet relations were at a low ebb in the early 1960s, and during the first two years of Kennedy's Presidency there had been virtually no meaningful dialogue between the superpowers on issues that divided them, or on issues that united them. Among the most startling revelations of the [1987]

Cambridge conference, quite apart from the volume of hard data and informed opinion the Soviet participants provided, was the vast extent of the gulf between the view from Washington and the view from Moscow prior to the crisis, and how quickly a gulf of that kind can be narrowed if, in the serious and cooperative atmosphere that permeated the Cambridge conference itself, Americans and Soviets speak candidly and soberly about it.

4

"Thirteen Days": Its Relevance Today

Theodore C. Sorensen

Theodore C. Sorensen, a special adviser to President Kennedy and a member of the Executive Committee, believes that "presidential leadership" is the thing that counts most during critical times. He cites firmness, flexibility, and the willingness to maintain dialogue with the adversary as qualities that would achieve results. He advises that in a confrontation, a leader should opt for measured and limited steps to give the other side an option. Sorensen, whose book *Kennedy* is a standard account of the Kennedy presidency, currently practices international law in New York.

A recent bulletin from Washington reports that the Bush White House plans to screen the movie "13 Days," the real-life dramatization of John F. Kennedy's ultimately peaceful resolution of the Cuban missile crisis of October 1962. President Bush himself intends to watch it. Good.

The movie is not a documentary. For dramatization (and marketing) purposes, it inflates the role of appointments secretary Kenny O'Donnell, played by Kevin Costner, and shortchanges the contributions of Adlai Stevenson, McGeorge Bundy and Gen. Maxwell Taylor. But it is a vivid and valuable reminder that those thirteen days demonstrated seven basic truths for every future president:

• There is no substitute for presidential leadership, no matter how experienced and brilliant the president's top advisers may be. It is the president's own judgment, his own knowledge of his adversary and allies, and his ability to guide his advisers and weigh conflicting advice that matter most in the end.

• A negotiated solution, when possible and reasonable, always serves the interests of both parties better than a military solution, particularly in an age of proliferating weapons of mass destruction. Presidential firmness, flexibility and a willingness to maintain a confidential dialogue with the other side—even during the worst times of tension and confrontation—are indispensable.

• In world affairs, a U.S. president's every word to another nation's leader, whether written or spoken, private or public, is weighted with meaning and consequence. Drafting a letter that could mean the difference between life and death for one's countrymen, or even the planet, inspires clear and careful phrasing that leaves no loopholes but burns no bridges.

It is the president's own judgment . . . and his ability to guide his advisers and weigh conflicting advice that matter most in the end.

• When dealing with an aggressive adversary, a measured and limited first step that leaves both the president and the other side with an option other than humiliation or escalation is preferable to an unlimited surprise attack that invites both a belligerent response and the condemnation of history.

• A president's military advisers are likely to trust only military solutions; his diplomatic advisers are likely to see merit only in diplomatic solutions; his legal, economic and spiritual advisers are likely to focus primarily on the tools of their respective trades, etc. A presidential solution, possibly drawing upon the best elements of all the others, including a combination of fair-minded diplomacy with a threat of superior military force, is most often the right answer. Thrusting forward the olive branch and the arrows grasped by the eagle represented on the presidential seal requires an ambidextrous president with exquisite timing. But it sure beats the alternatives.

• For all the terrible power and deterrent value of nuclear missiles, our highly trained conventional forces, alerted and informed by a high-tech, highly skilled intelligence community, are the most likely and most practical weapons for a president to use in a military crisis.

• However slow and divided the United Nations Security Council may be at particular times, no one is better positioned to serve as an independent (not necessarily neutral) and invaluable channel of confidential communications and cool reflection than the secretary-general of that oft-maligned organization.

All these lessons and more come through in the movie as well as the published tape transcripts of that harrowing thirteen days. My role, as portrayed in the film and as transpired in 1962, was comparatively light. But the heavy sense of weight I felt when asked by the president to draft the penultimate letter to Soviet Chairman Nikita S. Khrushchev—with Atty. Gen. Robert Kennedy at my side, with anxious "hawks" and "doves" scratching for more, with nuclear war around the corner and one brave American U-2 pilot already down—was seared on my memory long before that moment was depicted on the screen. That was a moment that neither I nor any American would ever want to experience again.

Maybe the Bush team should see the movie twice.

Chronology

1957
The Soviet Union launches its first intercontinental ballistic missile (ICBM) in August and its first satellite, *Sputnik*, in October. Alarmed that the Soviet Union may have more nuclear weapons than what the military has estimated, the United States starts increasing its nuclear capability.

1959
Soviet Premier Nikita Khrushchev claims Soviet nuclear superiority over the United States. In Cuba, Fidel Castro assumes power after toppling the government of General Fulgencio Batista in a seven-year revolution.

October 1959
The United States and Turkey sign an agreement on the deployment of Jupiter nuclear missiles in Turkey. The missiles are part of a string of U.S. military installations in Europe meant to contain the USSR.

May 1960
The Soviet Union and Cuba establish diplomatic relations.

August–October 1960
The United States imposes an embargo on trade with Cuba. In response, Cuba nationalizes about $1 billion in U.S. private investments.

December 1960
Cuba formally aligns itself with the Soviet Union and indicates solidarity with the Sino-Soviet bloc.

January 1961
The United States and Cuba sever diplomatic relations. John F. Kennedy is inaugurated as the thirty-fifth president of the United States. In a speech to the Supreme Soviet, Premier Khrushchev once again asserts Soviet strategic superiority.

April 1961
Using Cuban exiles, the U.S. Central Intelligence Agency (CIA) launches an unsuccessful invasion of Cuba. Khrushchev assures Kennedy that the USSR will not establish mil-

itary bases in Cuba, but he warns against any more attacks on Cuba.

June 1961
In a meeting with Kennedy in Vienna, Khrushchev warns that the Soviet Union will cut Allied access to West Berlin.

August 1961
Soviet forces and East Germans erect the Berlin Wall, separating the Soviet-controlled east from the Allied-controlled west.

September–October 1961
U.S. intelligence discovers that Soviet capability for long-range missiles is much lower than earlier estimates. Deputy Secretary of Defense Roswell Gilpatric announces that America has a much larger nuclear arsenal than the Soviet Union.

November 1961
Kennedy announces that the country's stockpile of nuclear weapons is much more than the Soviet Union's. Kennedy also authorizes a $50-million covert program, Operation Mongoose, aimed at destabilizing and eventually overthrowing Castro.

April 1962
U.S. Jupiter missiles in Turkey become operational. Khrushchev explores deploying similar weapons in Cuba to increase Soviet nuclear capability and to deter U.S. invasion of Cuba.

May 1962
The Soviet military determines the composition of weapons to be sent to Cuba, which includes twenty-four medium-range ballistic missile (MRBM) launchers, sixteen intermediate-range (IRBM) launchers, four elite combat regiments, twenty-four surface-to-air missile (SAM) batteries, forty-two MiG-21 interceptors, forty-two IL-28 bombers, twelve Komar-class missile boats, and coastal defense cruise missiles. A Soviet delegation goes to Cuba to propose to Castro the deployment of missiles. Castro accepts the proposal.

July 1962
Raul Castro, Fidel's brother and Cuba's defense minister, visits the Soviet Union to discuss further the details of the missile deployment.

August 1962

Aleksandr Alekseyev, Soviet ambassador to Cuba, discusses with Castro the agreement governing the missile deployment. Castro introduces a few amendments. Che Guevarra and Emilio Aragones Navarro, close associates of Fidel Castro, meet with Khrushchev and urge him to announce the missile deployment publicly, but Khrushchev declines. U.S. intelligence reports Soviet weapons build-up in Cuba. Kennedy orders the drawing up of a contingency plan and the speeding up of Operation Mongoose to overthrow Castro.

September 1962

Soviet troops start arriving in Cuba. Kennedy and his advisers discuss the weapons build up in Cuba. The U.S. Air Force approves a plan for an air attack on Cuba in preparation for an invasion. Soviet ambassador Anatoly Dobrynin assures American officials that there are no offensive weapons in Cuba.

Early October 1962

Attorney General Robert Kennedy, the president's brother and close confidant, orders Operation Mongoose to intensify sabotage operations. The military directs increased readiness for an invasion of Cuba. At the U.N. General Assembly, Cuban president Dorticos warns that if Cuba is invaded, it will defend itself.

October 14

A U-2 aircraft obtains photographs that provide the first hard evidence of MRBM sites in Cuba.

October 15

The National Photographic Interpretation Center informs the CIA that photos show MRBM, SAM, and IL-28 sites in Cuba. The CIA informs White House officials about the discovery. A major military exercise, PHIBRIGLEX-62 is set to begin. The operation, involving twenty thousand navy personnel and four thousand marines, launches a mock assault on Puerto Rico's Vieques Island to overthrow a tyrant named "Ortsac"—*Castro* spelled backwards. The exercise is used as cover for increasing military readiness for a strike on Cuba.

October 16

McGeorge Bundy informs President Kennedy about the photos of Soviet MRBMs in Cuba. Kennedy convenes his advisers, who become the Executive Committee (ExCom). Discussions center on alternative courses of action: (1) political action or diplomacy, (2) a single, surgical air strike on the missile bases, (3) a comprehensive series of attacks and invasions, and (4) a blockade of Cuba.

October 17

To maintain secrecy, Kennedy follows his planned schedule, flying to Connecticut to campaign for Democratic Party candidates there. ExCom meets again to discuss options. The Joint Chiefs of Staff, especially the U.S. Air Force's commander, strongly argue for air strikes.

October 18

Kennedy meets with Soviet foreign minister Andrei Gromyko; he does not tell the latter that he knows about the missiles in Cuba. Gromyko asserts there are no offensive weapons in Cuba. ExCom meets and discusses the merits of air strikes versus a naval blockade.

October 19

Kennedy travels to the Midwest for another campaign trip. He asks ExCom to draw up plans for both air strikes and a naval blockade.

October 20

Kennedy cuts short his trip to meet with his advisers; he tends to favor limited action through a blockade.

October 21

ExCom advises Kennedy to use the word *quarantine*, instead of *blockade*, which would amount to a declaration of war. The press hounds the White House to issue statements on Cuba. Kennedy personally calls the *Washington Post* and the *New York Times* to ask them to tone down their coverage of Cuba for security reasons.

October 22

Kennedy addresses the nation on television, informing the American public about the missiles in Cuba, announcing the naval blockade, and warning the Soviet Union to remove the offensive weapons at once.

October 23

Khrushchev writes Kennedy, calling the blockade a "serious threat to peace" and insists that the weapons in Cuba are only for defense. U.S. representative Adlai Stevenson takes the case to the UN Security Council. Moscow places the armed forces of the Warsaw Pact countries on alert. Castro addresses the nation and mobilizes 270,000 armed men. He asserts that Cuba will not disarm while the United States persists to be hostile. Kennedy sends a message to Khrushchev urging him to order Soviet ships to observe the eight-hundred-mile quarantine zone. President Kennedy sends Robert Kennedy to meet with Ambassador Dobrynin to explore diplomatic ways of ending the crisis.

October 24

The blockade takes effect. Initially, sixteen out of nineteen Soviet ships reverse course and return to the Soviet Union, but two ships and a Soviet submarine approach the line. The three stop short of the quarantine zone. Secretary of State Dean Rusk observes, "We've been eyeball to eyeball and the other fellow just blinked." UN secretary general U Thant urges the two leaders to exercise restraint and calls for the suspension of arms shipments to Cuba and the naval quarantine. The U.S. military increases its highest alert for the first time in history. The Defense Department draws up civil defense preparations.

October 25

Kennedy sends a message to Khrushchev acknowledging the latter's letter of October 24. He repeats his demand that the Soviet government remove the missiles. The CIA reports that some of the missiles in Cuba are now operational. Influential columnist Walter Lippmann proposes that the United States remove the Jupiters from Turkey in return for the Soviet missiles in Cuba.

October 26

The construction of missile bases in Cuba continues. Kennedy orders the increase of low-level surveillance flights in Cuba to twelve a day and a program to establish a civilian government in Cuba after invasion. ExCom estimates 18,500 casualties during the first ten days of such an invasion. John Scali, State Department correspondent for ABC News, meets with Aleksandr Fomin, the Soviet embassy public affairs counselor, known to be the KGB's Washington station chief. Fomin proposes that the Soviet Union dismantle the bases, under UN supervision, in exchange for a

U.S. pledge not to invade Cuba. Scali brings the proposal to the State Department. U.S. officials assume Fomin had the authority from Khrushchev to make this offer. The State Department receives a proposal from Khrushchev: The Soviet Union will withdraw the missiles if the United States will declare it will not invade Cuba or support other forces hostile to Cuba. ExCom discusses Khrushchev's letter, alongside Fomin's proposal. Robert Kennedy and Dobrynin meet secretly again. Dobrynin brings up the missiles in Turkey, and Robert Kennedy offers to introduce them into a potential settlement. Castro transmits a cable to Khrushchev telling him an attack will occur in two or three days, and to preempt it, the Soviet Union should strike first. (Castro, in January 1992, denied this, saying his letter was mistranslated by Soviet ambassador Alekseyev. He said that he suggested that if Cuba were invaded, the Soviet Union would need to defend itself from attack by using nuclear weapons.) Castro orders commanders to open fire on all U.S. aircraft flying over the island. The U.S. military plan includes three massive air strikes a day to destroy Cuban air capability.

October 27
The CIA reports that three of the four MRBM sites appear to be operational. Castro intensifies mobilization of Cuban forces. At eleven in the morning, Khrushchev's second message is received at the White House. He adds a new condition to his first letter: The Soviet Union will remove the missiles in Cuba if the United States will remove its missiles in Turkey. Kennedy favors the proposal, saying that to choose war over the missile deal would be insupportable. Robert McNamara argues that the Jupiters should be removed in advance of an invasion. Maxwell Taylor, representing the Joint Chiefs of Staff, recommends air strikes and invasion. The State Department flatly rejects the Soviet proposal. A U-2 surveillance aircraft from a U.S. base in Alaska strays into Soviet airspace on what was reported to be a "routine air sampling mission." The pilot, after realizing his error, radios for help. A U.S. F-102 fighter in Alaska, armed with nuclear missiles, heads toward the Bering Sea. At the same time, Soviet MiGs take off to intercept the U-2, which manages to escape. Another incident occurs around noon. A U-2 plane is shot down over Cuba, killing its pilot. ExCom assumes that the move had been ordered by the

Kremlin and was meant to escalate the crisis. (Years later, Soviet and Cuban officials acknowledged it was local Soviet and Cuban officials who ordered the firing.) Kennedy orders the military not to retaliate. ExCom decides to respond to Khrushchev's first letter and to be silent on the Turkish missiles. Kennedy meets with a smaller group of advisers, which decides to send a message to Ambassador Dobrynin saying that if the missiles are not withdrawn, there will be military action. The message also states that if the missiles are removed, the United States will pledge not to invade Cuba and the missiles in Turkey will be removed once the crisis is over. The group agrees there will be no public disclosure of the deal over the Jupiters, and there should be no leak to the press about it. In the evening, Kennedy's letter to Khrushchev is transmitted to Moscow: The Soviet Union should remove the weapon systems from Cuba under the supervision of the United Nations. The United States—upon the establishment of appropriate arrangements through the UN—will lift the quarantine and give assurances against the invasion of Cuba. The message is released to the press to avoid communication delays. Castro writes U Thant that he will stop work in the missile sites once the United States lifts the blockade. He also extends an invitation to U Thant to visit Cuba. ExCom reviews options, including an air strike, extending the blockade to include petroleum, oil, and lubricants. In Cuba, Castro meets with Soviet ambassador Alekseyev in the evening. Alekseyev had earlier briefed Castro on the messages between Moscow and Washington. Castro calls the situation "highly alarming."

October 28

At nine in the morning, a new message from Premier Khrushchev is broadcast on Radio Moscow. The message: The Soviet Union has ordered the dismantling of the weapons and their return to the Soviet Union. Kennedy halts air missions during the day. Several of Kennedy's advisers are unconvinced by the Soviet statement. Admiral George Anderson complains, "We have been had." General Curtis LeMay suggests the United States launch air strikes right away. The military orders commanders not to relax their alert status. Castro goes into a rage over Khrushchev's decision, calling him a "son of a bitch," "bastard," and "lacking *cojones*" (balls). He declares the Kennedy-Khrushchev arrangement unsatisfactory and adds his "five-point" demand: (1) end the economic blockade against Cuba; (2) end all U.S. subversive activities against Cuba; (3) halt all attacks on Cuba carried out from U.S. military bases in Puerto Rico, (4) cease aerial and naval reconnaissance flights in Cuban airspace and waters, and (5) return Guantánamo naval base to Cuba. In the evening, Castro receives a telegram from the Kremlin explaining the decision to withdraw the missiles and stressing Soviet commitment to defend Cuba.

November 1962

The United States tells the USSR that the IL-28 bombers in Cuba are offensive weapons and should be removed. It also continues the naval blockade and the surveillance overflights. Khrushchev urges Kennedy to formalize the agreement on the noninvasion pledge, but Kennedy refuses. The U.S. military recommends taking out the IL-28s by an air attack. In mid-November Khrushchev and Castro finally agree to remove the IL-28s. The United States suspends the quarantine, and the military reduces its alert status. The Soviet Union and the Warsaw Pact nations cancel the military preparedness alert.

December 1962

Khrushchev urges a halt in nuclear experiments and tests. This leads to the eventual signing of a limited test-ban treaty in August 1963.

January 1963

Turkey announces that the Jupiter missiles will be phased out. The U.S. military also announces that the Jupiters in Italy will be removed soon. The last missile in Turkey is dismantled on April 25. Kennedy continues to refuse to issue a formal non-invasion pledge, claiming the inspection, which is part of the settlement, has not happened. The CIA continues programs aimed at destabilizing Castro and his government.

April–May 1963

Castro meets with Khrushchev during a fourteen-day visit to the Soviet Union. For the first time, Castro learns that the Jupiters in Turkey were part of the agreement.

For Further Research

Books

Graham T. Allison, *Essence of Decision: Explaining the Cuban Missile Crisis*. Boston: Little, Brown, 1971.

Irving Bernstein, *Promises Kept: John F. Kennedy's New Frontier*. New York: Oxford University Press, 1991.

James G. Blight and David A. Welch, *On the Brink: Americans and Soviets Reexamine the Cuban Missile Crisis*. New York: Random House, 1991.

Dino A. Burgioni, *Eyeball to Eyeball: The Inside Story of the Cuban Missile Crisis*. Ed. Robert F. McCort. New York: Random House, 1991.

Laurence Chang and Peter Kornbluh, eds., *The Cuban Missile Crisis, 1962: A National Security Archive Documents Reader*. New York: New Press, 1998.

Raymond L. Garthoff, *Reflections on the Cuban Missile Crisis*. Rev. ed. Washington, DC: Brookings Institution, 1989.

Roger Hilsman, *To Move a Nation: The Politics of Foreign Policy in the Administration of JFK*. Garden City, NY: Doubleday, 1967.

Robert F. Kennedy, *Thirteen Days: A Memoir of the Cuban Missile Crisis*. New York: Norton, 1969.

Nikita Khrushchev, *Khrushchev Remembers: The Glasnost Tapes*. Trans. and ed. Jerrold L. Schecter with Vyacheslav V. Luchkov. Boston: Little, Brown, 1990.

Walter LaFeber, *America, Russia, and the Cold War*. 3rd ed. New York: John Wiley and Sons, 1976.

David L. Larson, ed., *The Cuban Crisis of 1962: Selected Documents, Chronology, and Bibliography*. 2nd ed. Lanham, MD: University Press of America, 1986.

Richard Ned Lebow and Janice Gross Stein, *We All Lost the Cold War*. Princeton, NJ: Princeton University Press, 1994.

Ernest R. May and Philip D. Zelikow, eds., *The Kennedy Tapes: Inside the White House During the Cuban Missile*

119

Crisis. Cambridge, MA: Belknap Press of Harvard University Press, 1997.

James Nathan, ed., *The Cuban Missile Crisis Revisited*. New York: St. Martin's, 1992.

Arthur M. Schlesinger Jr., *A Thousand Days: JFK in the White House*. Boston: Houghton, Mifflin, 1965.

Theodore C. Sorensen, *Kennedy*. New York: Harper & Row, 1965.

I.F. Stone, *In Time of Torment*. New York: Random House, 1967.

Robert Smith Thompson, *Missiles of October*. New York: Simon & Schuster, 1992.

Mark J. White, *Missiles in Cuba: Kennedy, Khrushchev, Castro, and the 1962 Crisis*. Chicago: Ivan R. Dee, 1997.

Periodicals

Daniel Ellsberg, "The Day Castro Almost Started World War III," *New York Times*, October 31, 1987.

David Lowenthal, "U.S. Cuban Policy: Illusion and Reality," *National Review*, January 29, 1963.

Richard Reeves, "Call 'Days' What You Will, but It's Not Quite History," *Los Angeles Times*, January 16, 2001.

Claude Sitton, "Southeast, Nearest Cuba, Feels Impact of Crisis," *New York Times*, October 26, 1962.

Theodore C. Sorensen, "The 'Thirteen' Days Taught Seven Truths," *Los Angeles Times*, February 1, 2001.

Tim Weiner, "When Kennedy Faced Armageddon, and His Own Scornful Generals," *New York Times*, October 5, 1997.

Internet Sources

Marxists Internet Archive, "Cuban History: Missile Crisis." www.marxists.org/history/cuba/subject/missile-crisis/index.htm.

Kurt Weirsma and Ben Larson, "The Cuban Missile Crisis." www.library.thinkquest.org/11046/days/index.html.

Index